D1564014

THE PARADOX OF LOVE

PASCAL BRUCKNER

Translated by STEVEN RENDALL

and with an afterword by

RICHARD GOLSAN

The Paradox of Love

PRINCETON UNIVERSITY PRESS
Princeton and Oxford

Originally published in France as *Le Paradoxe Amoureux*
© Grasset & Fasquelle, Paris, 2009

Copyright © 2012 by Princeton University Press
Requests for permission to reproduce material from this work should be sent
to Permissions, Princeton University Press
Published by Princeton University Press, 41 William Street,
Princeton, New Jersey 08540
In the United Kingdom: Princeton University Press, 6 Oxford Street,
Woodstock, Oxfordshire OX20 1TW

press.princeton.edu

Library of Congress Cataloging-in-Publication Data

Bruckner, Pascal.
    [Paradoxe amoureux. English]
    The paradox of love Pascal Bruckner ; translated by Steven Rendall.
        p.   cm.
    Includes bibliographical references and index.
    ISBN 978-0-691-14914-1 (hardcover : alk. paper)   1. Love.
2. Man-woman relationships.   I. Title.
    HQ801.B873513 2011
    306.709'03—dc23

                                        2011028357
British Library Cataloging-in-Publication Data is available

Cet ouvrage a bénéficié du soutien des Programmes d'aide à la publication
de Culturesfrance/Ministère français des affaires étrangères et européennes.

This work, published as part of a program of aid for publication, received
support from CulturesFrance and the French Ministry of Foreign Affairs.

Ouvrage publié avec le concours du Ministère français chargé de la culture—
Centre National du Livre.

This work is published with support from the French Ministry of Culture/
Centre National du Livre.

This book has been composed in Minion

Printed on acid-free paper. ∞

Printed in the United States of America

10 9 8 7 6 5 4 3 2 1

Contents

♥

Introduction

Paris, early 1970s: On the Left Bank, in the Mouffetard neighborhood, an alternative preschool had opened up. It was founded on the assumption that education should be free of charge, seek the full development of children, and involve the participation of parents. I took my son there every day. Over the months, the project fell apart: The adults hung around on the second floor making love or smoking joints, leaving the kids to themselves. The big kids tormented the little ones until they sobbed, and none of them had their noses or their bottoms wiped. Play equipment and pharmaceuticals regularly disappeared. The few fathers and mothers who actually performed their assigned tasks at the school started withdrawing their children and putting them back in schools run by "the bourgeois capitalist state." The alternative preschool had become a shambles and, after a few final quarrels, closed its doors.

Shortly afterward, I went to Christiana, a free commune in Copenhagen, Denmark: At a dinner in this sentimental kolkhoz, attended by a few dozen strapping fellows who looked like Christ and their female companions, all with long blond hair, adorable little boys and girls danced on the table, shouted, fought, trampled on the food, and threw cheese, mashed potatoes, and ham at each other amid their impassive parents, who were too busy puffing on their pot

1

pipes or snuggling with one another to offer the slightest re-
proof. When the chaos had become unbearable, the adults
left the table, leaving the battlefield to the kids, who were
disappointed not to have been reprimanded. A good wallop
would have seemed completely out of place.

The 1960s and 1970s left those who lived through them
with the memory of an immense generosity combined with
candor and a profound silliness. We thought our potential
was unlimited: no prohibition, no illness stood in our way.
Economic prosperity, the collapse of already worm-eaten
taboos, the feeling of being a predestined generation in an
abominable century—all these led to a multitude of projects. We nourished the dream of an absolute break with the
past; from one day to the next the world would turn into an
inconceivable Eden, and the very meanings of words would
change. We were going to put centuries of distance between
ourselves and our ancestors, and there was no question of
following in their footsteps. Sexual liberation became the
most common way of getting in contact with the extraordinary: every morning we reinvented our lives, we traveled
from bed to bed even more easily than we traveled over the
surface of the globe, willing partners awaited us everywhere,
even in the most distant lands. Our freedom, intoxicated
with itself, no longer knew any bounds, the world loved us
and we loved it back. The age invited us to give free rein
to our appetites, and happiness consisted in multiplying
our passions, finding ways to satisfy them immediately.
Everyone wanted to be a pioneer, to deny himself or herself
nothing, to pursue fantasies to the very end. In these years
of innocence, there was an unparalleled creativity and an in-
credible fecundity in the areas of art, music, and literature.

What put an end to this euphoria? The emergence of AIDS, the cruelty of capitalism, the return of a moral order? It was simply that time went on. We knew only one season in life: eternal youth. Life played a terrible trick on us: we got old. The movement, having accomplished its role in history, ran out of steam. It was less a revolution than the culmination of a process that had begun much earlier. The taboos that had been uprooted didn't come back on us like weeds. Some achievements of this period remain unchallenged: the change in the condition of women, contraception, divorce, the decriminalization of abortion, the second sex's massive entry into the world of work. Above all, the sixties and seventies gave birth to a conceptual oddity: "free love." The expression had long meant promiscuity, the circulation of bodies, easy lays. Now we have to understand it at a higher level as the oxymoron par excellence, the improbable union of belonging and independence, a new system that affects us all, whatever our milieu, our opinions, our inclinations. How can love, which attaches, be compatible with freedom, which separates?

The field of love is divided between two great discourses that pass through multiple channels: the discourse of lament and the discourse of subversion. For the former, the truth of love was lost somewhere between the troubadours and the Romantics; for the latter, it is still to come, when humanity, having rid itself of its bourgeois trappings, has broken its last chains. This gives rise to two contradictory projects: restoring and overthrowing. Erasing the accursed parenthesis of the sixties, rehabilitating the traditional family, repealing the rights accorded women, or, inversely, doing away with the couple and jealousy, throwing them in the ashcan of History. Thus we are called upon to be archaic or modern, caged or free. As if love were a disease and we had to drop everything else to cure ourselves of it, as if we had to excuse ourselves for loving the way we do.

It has to be admitted that in this domain the effort to wipe the slate clean has failed: neither marriage, the family, nor the demand for fidelity has disappeared. But the ambition to return to the *status quo ante* has also failed. Even the most retrograde have been affected by the upheaval. People are astonished by, and often regret, what is new in our morals; inversely, I am astonished by how much our morals have remained the same, despite so many changes. For a generation that wanted to reform the human heart, it has been a strange experience to rediscover certain inviolable codes. Today, the ideas of revolution and restoration are disappearing in favor of a complex, sedimented conception of a time that is neither a return to the past nor the advent of a new era. Less a transcendence than a displacement.

This book was written for those who reject the choice between revolution and restoration, who refuse to abandon the old drama of the passions but do not disavow the changes that have occurred. Unlike the conservatives, they celebrate the rights achieved, but unlike the progressives, they do not feel guilty about their old-fashioned tastes. To tell the truth, at the height of the lyrical years the old world that we claimed to be escaping had already caught up with us. We were thwarted libertines, romantic philanderers, sentimental hedonists, caught between two masters: constancy and inconstancy.

Our freedom in love was won in battle at a price that remains to be determined. (Someday the "black book" of the

1960s will have to be written.) Freedom does not release us from responsibilities but instead increases them. It does not lighten our burden but weighs us down further. It resolves problems less than it multiplies paradoxes. If this world sometimes seems brutal, that is because it is "emancipated" and each individual's autonomy collides with that of others and is injured by them: never have people had to bear on their shoulders so many constraints. This burden explains in part why contemporary romances are so hard.

A paradoxical result: we now ask everything from love; we ask too much of it; we ask that it ravish, ravage, and redeem us. It is assigned such a grandiose ambition in no culture other than ours. Christianity's invention of the God of love has made the virtue of love the cardinal value of life. Countless forms of messianism derived from Christianity, notably communism, have in turn raised love to the pinnacle, with varying outcomes, thereby proving that sentiment, once it is demanded by a state or an institution, is as dangerous as an explosive. By liberating itself, it reveals itself for what it is, in its flashes of brilliance and in its pettiness: noble and base at the same time.

PART I

A Great Dream of Redemption

CHAPTER 1

Liberating the Human Heart

I have loved women to the point of madness. But I
have always preferred my liberty.

GIACOMO CASANOVA*

God, how I loved my freedom before I began to
love you more than I loved it. How it weighs on me
today!

GUY DE MAUPASSANT, *Fort comme la mort*

In 1860, when as an opponent of Napoleon III he was living
in exile on the island of Guernsey in the English Channel,
Victor Hugo associated freedom of thought with freedom
in love in a new way: "One corresponds to the heart, the
other to the mind: they are the two sides of freedom of con-
science. No one has the right to ask which God I believe
in or which woman I love, and the law less than anyone."[1]
Further on in the same text, he protested against bourgeois
marriage: "You love a man other than your husband? Well
then, go to him. If you do not love a man, you are his whore;
if you love a man, you are his wife. In sexual union, the

Translator's note: Unless otherwise noted, all translations are my own.

heart is the law. Love and think freely. The rest concerns only God."[2] Hugo praises adultery as an unauthorized but legitimate protest against matrimonial despotism that allows a woman to escape the tomb of an undesired marriage.[3]

Love Has to Be Reinvented (Arthur Rimbaud)

Here Hugo takes his place in the genealogy of rebels who from the eighteenth century to the end of the twentieth sought to situate love in the great saga of emancipation, from the philosophers of the Enlightenment to Wilhelm Reich, by way of the utopian writer Charles Fourier, the anarchists, surrealism, and the whole hippie movement of "Flower Power." Enlightenment thinkers believed that it was possible to reconcile love with virtue, the pleasure of the body with the elevation of the soul: anyone who is capable of loving is capable of grandeur and of leading others along the path of progress. For Rousseau, for example, reciprocity and the transparency of consciences necessarily symbolized to the highest degree human excellence, morality, and communion. And if in *The New Heloise* he argues against gallantry and the affectations of politeness, it is only to restore to affective impulses their absolute innocence. This myth of the perfect love that "raises human love above humanity" (Bernardin de Saint-Pierre) gathered unprecedented speed with the events of 1789, at least at first.

The French Revolution sought to start over on new bases, even if in order to do so it might prove necessary to "purge even the heart," as a man called Billaud-Varennes demanded in the month of Floreal of Year III.[4] Doing violence to nature, taking the scalpel even to our innermost code, had been the ambition of all reformers for the past two centuries: regenerating love and regenerating true love. Stripping it of the veils that made it ugly in order to restore it to its first function: making the human race a single, passionately united family. Here we are in the register of the radiant promise that Rousseau often made when he predicted happy days for mothers who agreed to nurse their children:

> I dare promise these worthy mothers a solid and constant attachment on the part of their husbands, a truly filial tenderness on the part of their children, the esteem and respect of the public, a successful confinement without problems and without after-effects, and sound and vigorous health. . . . If mothers consent to nurse their children, morals will be reformed by themselves, natural sentiments will reawaken in every heart, the state will be repopulated.[5]

After the condemnation of passion in the classical age— "love alone is more to be feared than all shipwrecks," Fénelon says in his *Télémaque*—the eighteenth century invented the revolution of private life. A new phenomenon emerged: the bonds between parents and children grew steadily stronger. The family became a laboratory of sentiment and was also about to become the foundation of the social contract.[6] Freed from the dross with which earlier periods had burdened it, the family was expected to become a virtue that would raise the human race from barbarism to civilization.

In the latter half of the twentieth century, this will to re-create man and society from top to bottom gained the aid of sexuality, which some regarded as a complementary remedy, and others as a substitute remedy. That is where we are today: for the past two centuries, Western culture has sought to build "a repair workshop for humanity" (Francis Ponge) and to restore to love its true face, to make it the basis for a society of brothers and lovers. Here we will recount the episodes of this mad attempt.

Salvation through Orgasm

In opposition to bourgeois pettiness and Romantic prudishness, a twofold counterattack: that of a single passion and that of joyous promiscuity. On the one hand, in 1884 Engels predicted (in his book *The Origins of the Family, Private Property, and the State*) the triumph of a happy monogamy, promoted by proletarian revolution, that would sweep away the enslavement of women and its corollaries, adultery and prostitution. On the other hand, the French anarchist Émile Armand defended, even before 1914, the idea of an "amorous comradeship" free of hypocrisy and jealousy and based on sexual pluralism.[7]

The aspiration to develop a new education of the human race by combining hygiene, pleasure, and inclination then emerged: the goal was to free the body from control by the church and by capital, to shield it from the depressing sermons of the priests, from the exhausting pace set by the bosses, from the tyranny of the clock. Here again it was a question of moving "the borderline between the possible and the impossible" (Mona Ozouf) and reestablishing nudity in its prelapsarian innocence. According to the early Christians, sexuality was an animal that had to be chained up; now it is a fabulous animal that has to be freed. At the foundation of this aspiration, which extends from certain religious heresies to the feminist and socialist movements, there is a certitude that desire is good, that it alone is capable of stripping society of its ugly aspects. It was of course with Freud, who revealed the carnal foundation of our civilizations, with Herbert Marcuse, who went to teach in the United States, and especially with Wilhelm Reich, a physician who rebelled against psycho-analysis and the German Communist Party and died in the United States in 1957, that this militant effort of Promethean reconstruction reached its apogee. Refusing to distinguish between social revolution and personal revolution, main-taining that "sexual life is not a private matter,"[8] Reich, a victim of both Nazism and Stalinism, sought throughout his life the best way of escaping from "the human servile structure." Only a full aptitude for pleasure makes it pos-sible to reconcile humans with themselves and allows them to rid themselves of the infantile derivatives constituted by pornography, detective novels, horror stories, and especially submission to the leader, all of which are connected with fear, that is, with frustration. "Authoritarian, mechanistic civiliza-tion," religious mysticism, and bourgeois repression build up around every individual an "emotional armor" that kills joy in life and stunts people. Since relief from tensions in the erotic convulsion is the very formula of the living being (the Aurora Borealis is nothing other than a cosmic orgasm), it alone should put an end "to blind obedience to the Fuhrer," and lead to the gradual disappearance of possessiveness, can-cer, dictatorship, and violence.

Properly understood, the sexual revolution is not an al-leviation of sexual problems: it inserts a historical break that causes us to move, as Marxists would say, from prehistory to history. With Wilhelm Reich, we are dealing with a biological utilitarianism based on a metaphysics of salvation: like grace for the Calvinists, the orgasm is the narrow gate to redemption. The liquidating power it implies constitutes the panacea that is supposed to protect us from all political or physical epidemics: "the people's sexual happiness is the best guarantee of the security of society as a whole."[9] Since our bodies are our only homeland, and since they are inseparable, as they were among the Greeks, from the cosmos and from climatic changes, a fundamental game is played out in the bellies of men and women. It is up to you to make the body a garden of delights or a hell of repression: because the bioenergy that runs through us in spasms is exactly the same as the one that animates living matter and the movement of the stars. (Reich, exiled to America at the end of his life, where he was persecuted by the FBI, constructed strange machines for capturing "orgonic" radiations, including a device for breaking up clouds that succeeded in producing rain in the desert.) Depending on whether or not you have an orgasm, the Earth will slip into harmony or into discord: Fourier had already drawn an analogy between human copulation and that of the planets, and saw in the Milky Way an immense deposit of luminous semen. If humans made love more enthusiastically, they would give birth to a multitude of galaxies that would illuminate the planet *a giorno* and would solve the lighting problem at small expense. Sade himself compared orgasm to a volcanic eruption and the apathy of the libertine to cold blocks of lava after the explosion.

In the 1960s, which rediscovered these authors (along with the inspiration of certain millenarian sects), sex became demonstrative, assigned a messianic status: what speaks through it in a confused way is neither more nor less than the human enigma. The disturbances of Eros cannot be reduced to a surge of shameless behavior, as the prudish claimed; they corresponded to an "uprising in the soul," as the great historian Denis de Rougemont had already noted in 1961. The goal was to re-create paradise using the instruments of decline itself, to fabricate a new Eve, a new Adam. Our ancestors murmured what we are finally saying clearly; the best among them were precursors, and we are now entering into the kingdom, into maturity of humanity. Our shameful parts have now become our glorious parts, but also our warlike parts. An erection is an insurrection, the body in emotional turmoil overthrows the diktats issued by the established order, desire is profoundly moral. There is no need to resort to the old Freudian concept of sublimation, the instincts are sublime in themselves and include the totality of the human condition; since evil had its origins in psychological drives, we were going to become good by making love. Coitus is simultaneously a rebellion against society and the culmination of human nature. This claim made by the prophets of liberation, that they were acting at the very source of sentiment, explains both their excitement and their belligerent tone.

This period revived the suspicion, which had already been aroused by the Enlightenment, that love is only a mask for desire, a lie that people tell each other in order to disguise their lust. "Love no longer exists," Robert Musil had already said, "all that remains is sexuality and comradeship." For their part, Gilles Deleuze and Félix Guattari pointed to "the ignoble desire to be loved." Indicted, sentiment would be acquitted by desire on the condition that it give up its pre-eminence and be content with a small role in the new scenario that was being written. Thus the ancient expression "I love you" had to be banned and the only authentic one—"I want you"—substituted for it. Praise for the naked human being reduced to itself, to its most precious possession: the body, the only reality in a materialism properly understood. Since repression provokes neuroses and pathologies, license can never be sufficiently licentious. No excess committed by the children of May 1968 could compare in ugliness with the hideous restrictions imposed by their parents. Whence the tolerance of those years with regard to all forms of attraction, including incest and pedophilia, and the certitude that children also have a right to sexuality, even with adults. The irenicism of childish speech concealed practices that were less irenic. In the same breath an attempt was made to wrench love away from domestic imprisonment and reshape the family and education. Anyone who found ancient customs charming was accused of treachery. No doubt was permitted: the age had found the solution to emotional suffering and secondarily to social suffering.

The 1960s and 1970s were a sententious revolution, like the libertine novels of the eighteenth century: in them, the various forms of eroticism and perversion were transformed into revolutionary ideas, directed against the established order. The quasi-religious ambition of this period has been underestimated; it sought both to make outmoded the pitiful sentimental comedy found in Racine or Proust, and to embark upon an adventure unlike any other. Regarding the Paris commune and May 1968, André Malraux spoke of a "fanatical idyllism," a will to reconcile people with one another even at the price of violence. In fact, after those days we emerged into the era of "everything is political" and the comical habit, which is still alive today, of bringing the distinction between left and right even into the bedroom: the missionary position and prostitution are right-wing, sodomy and civil unions are left-wing! The central belief of this period persuaded of its superiority was that there is no tragedy, there are only bad social constructions. (Ideological constructivism is the very gospel of Western thought, perceptible today in the theory of genders.) The 1960s and 1970s were marked by the worship of the idealism of Eros, magnificent, and necessarily magnificent as soon as it ceased to be stifled by censorship, priests, political commissars, and the bourgeoisie. Thus we find praise for "the libidinal economy" (Jean-François Lyotard) and "desiring machines" (Deleuze, Guattari) in which everyone seeks her truth. A fundamental reversal: sexual pleasure, which was suspect, becomes obligatory, and anyone who escapes it is suspected of being seriously ill. A new terrorism of the orgasm replaces the old prohibitions.[10] For the ancients, Eros was a God; we moderns expect Eros to make us gods.

A certain qualification is needed, however. An unbiased reading of the Marquis de Sade, whose works were finally published *in extenso* during those years, might have tempered the ardor of our zealots: that fallen aristocrat, that incorrigible rake who, from the Old Regime to the Napoleonic Empire, spent twenty-seven years of his life in prison, never ceased in all his novels to show emancipated desire tending irresistibly toward arbitrariness, brutality, and mass crime. The true scandal of Sade, that great black pennant affixed to the Enlightenment's flag, is not his mad lubricity, it is his pessimism, his baleful way of confirming what religion has always said, namely that sex, far from being neutral, leads straight to cruelty. "There is no man who does not want to become a despot when he gets a hard-on," says a character in *The Philosopher in the Boudoir*. Sade alone seems to have understood the injunction "enjoy without fetters" as it should be understood: enjoy to the point of annihilating the other. In Europe, it is with Sade that sex became legislative, associating erotic license with political anarchy, but in his case it is a legislation put in the service of the strong in order to crush the weak and to allow the former to make use of the latter as they saw fit until they were exterminated. In thrall to its euphoria, the 1960s, not heeding the work of writers like Georges Bataille and Maurice Blanchot, produced nothing but pious readings of the "divine marquis," promoted to the rank of a subtle arranger of baroque syntactical periods or a precious precursor of the nice long-haired people who copulated amid smoke from joints and the vibrations of intoxicating music.

The Cunning of Sentimental Reason

We are the perplexed heirs of these traditions to which we owe so much. Without these pioneers, these sublime madmen who paid for their audacity with imprisonment, exile, and banishment, we would not be where we are. The 1960s will remain the decade of experimentation, of the invention of new possibilities of life through music, drugs, and travel. If the right to examine our heritage obtains in this domain more than in any other, we must first challenge an absolute contradiction: sentiment not only survived its condemnation by the supporters of a fanatical Eros but also emerged stronger than ever. In May 1968, the future Cardinal Lustiger, who was then an abbé, went to the Sorbonne, which was bubbling over. Revolted by the hullabaloo, the young priest is supposed to have said: "there is nothing evangelical in this chaos." It is possible to think that on the contrary, as Maurice Clavel and his friends saw, May 1968 was at bottom a spiritual insurrection that reactivated the dream of redeeming the world through kindness and solidarity. Clavel used the very eloquent metaphor of the wide-open faucet that a finger is trying to plug: the faucet is the Holy Spirit, the finger is the forces of reaction, the splatters are the miraculous consequences of this confrontation. We must never take at face value the discourses of actors participating in an event. May 1968 was no more a proletarian revolution than it was a desiring revolution. Just as it spoke Bolshevism in order to complete the erosion of communism, it celebrated radiant desire only in order to allow the triumph of an evangelical love that was entirely incarnate: a deepening and not a regression. The heart became flesh the better to unfold itself.

That is the cunning of amorous reason: each generation can play only a limited historical role before seeing its acts and its intentions turn against it and escape it. The enemies of the lie of sentiment were, despite themselves, the artisans of its restoration. By rehabilitating sexuality, May 1968 opened up a new career for love as a whole. It is impossible to maintain, as Roland Barthes did in 1977, that love was outlawed in relation to sex, or to explain with a touch of coquetry: "*Nous deux* [*We Two*, a magazine] is more obscene than the Marquis de Sade."[11] It was less love that was condemned than the patriarchal order's manipulation of it to keep women hidden. The mask was castigated, not the ideal of intimacy. The libidinal rhetoric, in its most excessive aspects, completed the sacralization of the affects that survived their programmed extinction.

Love was thus freed as one might free a sleeping princess. But the individual was also freed from the dross of traditions, religion, the family. These two liberations are in fact inseparable: as soon as the private individual is freed from collective control, as soon as he is offered, by being salaried, a little autonomy, he can finally take an interest in the quality of his emotions, and develop them as he wishes. He can give priority to the heart over the law of the clan and consider community pressures null and void. That is how the sentimental revolution in Europe began, partly thanks to nascent capitalism. For the first time, the masses had a right to enjoy the noble passions that had previously been reserved for princes and poets. Love is free only in a society of free individuals. But then we arrive at an aporia. Freedom can mean independence (not being subject to any authority), availability (remaining open to all opportunities), sovereignty (imposing one's will on others), or responsibility (assuming the consequences of one's acts). Now, three of these modalities contradict the type of relationship implied by life in a couple. Today, we are all, men and women, subjected to a contradictory requirement: to love passionately, and if possible to be loved, while at the same time remaining autonomous—to be free but cared for, with the hope that the couple will prove to be flexible enough to allow this harmonious coexistence.

I ask the other to give up willingly his or her own freedom, and I agree to do the same. But I am a cunning captive who constantly wants to take himself back. If the pleasure of love consists in no longer belonging to oneself, the pleasure of the self is never to abandon oneself. This is a tragicomic formula that the contemporary novel has exploited over and over: that of men or women who want to feel the great thrill without losing themselves and who fear that they will be cheated. Whence the dread of interpersonal relationships among modern couples who are in search of themselves, who flee each other, in a ballet of passionate commitments and abrupt retreats. "Free together," as a sociologist, François de Singly, has nicely put it in speaking of modern marriage: yes to the security of the home provided that it in no way prevents the full development of each partner. At the beginning of the twentieth century, Robert Musil already noted the importance that the word *partner* had acquired as a substitute for *husband* and *wife*: it designated a contractual relationship that can be dissolved by mutual consent. The influence of the economic model: each individual has now become her own little business, affairs of the heart are a subdivision of business affairs in general. And all the more because emancipation has increased the burden with new constraints—especially for women, who are expected to succeed in their professional, conjugal, and maternal lives. Intimate personal relations are modeled on labor relations: the return on investment has to be maximal. This free-market management is what gives modern stories their bitterness. A delicate mixture of reticence and sacrifice. The dream of a human relationship that would never go too far: I like you, I take you, you bore me, I leave you. One tries out the other as one would a new product.

Every person in love thus speaks two languages, that of a predestined attachment and that of free control over oneself. It is the superposition of these two languages that makes current relationships seem to be romances that are simultaneously lively and monotone: in Paris, two marriages in three end in divorce, and in the provinces, one in two; blended families are becoming more numerous. Every love affair is seen as both a stroke of good luck and a suffocating cage that deprives us of ourselves. The contemporary demand is that simultaneously we expose and preserve ourselves. The cultivation of pleasures has become an obsessive addiction. A hypoactive sexuality is one illness, a hyperactive sexuality is another. From the cigarette to the computer, everything provides an opportunity for detecting a pathological dependency. The schizophrenia of a period that preaches both enjoyment and mistrust, and that conceives the relation to the other on the model of drug addiction. Instead of emancipating ourselves together, as in the 1960s, we seek first of all to free ourselves from each other.

Contradictory Injunctions

The individual's dilemma: He would like to be his own foundation, but anxiously seeks the approval of those around him. He would like to be able to say, with the ex-Yippie Jerry Rubin: "I have to love myself enough not to need others to be happy." An improbable formula that recalls another by the French economist Léon Walras: "To be free is to feel oneself free of all others." Solipsism does not work or if it does, it frequently fails. The claim that one does not need anyone goes hand in hand with the bleak recognition that no one needs us, pride in self-sufficiency with the dread of being alone, the aspiration to distinguish oneself with a frenetic imitation of others. That is the misanthrope's torment: practicing seduction through invective, seeking people's approval while at the same time despising them, concealing her excessive desire for company in the guise of distancing herself. She has to be in the world in order to reject it, and if the world turns its back on her, she sees in this coolness the proof that her diagnosis is correct and prophesies the wickedness of the masses.

We are free, in democracies at least, to love whomever we choose and to embrace the sexuality of our choice, but there comes a time when we have to take the risk of a relationship to the other that will upset our expectations and free us from the dreary conversation with ourselves. Independence is not the last word for people—that is what we are told by the love that has a blind faith in the other: that is why the worst misfortune on Earth is the death of the few people who are dear to us and without whom life no longer has meaning or savor. But love is not the last word of human destiny either, if it means boredom and unhappiness—that is what individualism tells us. We are constantly struggling with these two injunctions, confusing freedom of choice in love, an immense progress, with the choice of individual freedom. In the first case, a conjugal solidarity is developed that transcends the insular self of each of the spouses; in the second case, we put the I before the We, at the risk of juxtaposing two solitudes. If there is a modern dream (old as the hills but widely shared today), it consists entirely in this twofold aspiration: to enjoy symbiosis with the other while at the same time remaining master of one's own life.

To this we must add the desire not to lose any of the friendships of childhood and adolescence, as is shown by American television series such as *Friends* or *Sex in the City*, communities of friends who prefer a multitude of affective bonds to the singleness of the bond of love. The persistence of the old gang in adulthood, a refusal to see work life break it up upon leaving high school or university. We want to keep these little groups bound together, groups that remain the depositories of a memory of solidarity and of escapades, and that refute the opposition between the best friend and the legitimate spouse or vice versa. Love is an experience we don't want to forego, on the condition that it not deprive us of any other experience. In short, like big children, we want everything and its opposite: we want to remain connected without being attached to anyone, and technology favors this. The telephone is a spouse for single people, allowing them to be with everyone without having to be close to anyone. The ways of overcoming solitude, such as the Internet and cell phones, are first of all ways of confirming it, because they make it tolerable.

Take the famous claim that "My body belongs to me." There is no more correct statement on the part of women, whom the dominant order has always deprived of free control over themselves and who want to make their own choices regarding love and motherhood. But if my body belongs to me, if no one wants it, what good is the title to this property? To the misfortune of being treated as a sexual object to be used in any way corresponds that other misfortune of never being awaited or desired. We begin by claiming a full and fierce sovereignty over ourselves that ends up weighing on us if no one calls upon us. We are thus absurdly expected either to preserve our freedom to lose love or renounce our freedom to preserve love.

The Old World Is Not Dead

Freer morals have thus favored women's liberation, bodies circulate more easily so long as they are "desirable," and information about sex is provided at an early age, along with the necessary warnings about sexually transmissible diseases. Marriage for love is widespread, though with shocking exceptions in areas still subject to patriarchal traditions; people can choose to continue or recommence their love lives even in old age; and minorities have recognized rights and show themselves without shame, at least in urban centers. In all honesty, however, we must admit that the old world has not had its last word: emancipation has not made contemporary erotic life less problematic; it has deteriorated into anxiety, pornographic commerce, and therapy. Love remains an enchanted village from which the elderly, the ugly, the deformed, and the poor are excluded. The crisis in male identity has diminished the power of the first sex only slightly, while the tyranny of appearances and youth is stronger than ever, and biological constraints continue to weigh on us, making motherhood difficult for women over forty, whereas men can fertilize eggs right up to the end of their lives. No matter how we look at it, "fishing for a husband" is as prevalent in the twenty-first century as it was in the sixteenth, while *homogamy* (intermarriage within a single group) remains preponderant, and money continues surreptitiously to impose its law in intimate relationships: it appears that more than 90 percent of women would like to marry or live with men who are older, more educated, and wealthier,[12] and the economically weak are not regarded as good marriage prospects. More than ever, power and money are erotic forces, and the fairy tale remains very close to the bank account: we find our loves chiefly in our own class and milieu, or if possible in a higher one.

In short, the desire for reform in matters of love collides with the old stuff of which human beings are made, and tough luck for those who wanted to make it the agent of spiritual progress. Whether we like it or not, to fall in love is to slip back into an ancient, magical humus, to revive childhood fears, excessive hopes, and a mixture of servitude and cruelty.[13] Without this permanence, how could we still read *The Princess of Cleves, Liaisons dangereuses, The Sufferings of Young Werther, Wuthering Heights, Cousin Bette, Madame Bovary,* or *In Search of Lost Time*? To understand the contemporary world, one can refer to Sade, Fourier, Reich, and Marcuse; we would also have to include Marx and Balzac, who saw in sex, power, and money the bourgeoisie's holy trinity, and render his due to Schopenhauer, who described sentiment as a trick played by nature to perpetuate the species. (Conversely, it can be maintained that the species is a trick played by love to superimpose itself on the blind mechanisms of reproduction.) After half a century of flamboyant discourses, what we find is the continuity of genetic, social, and political laws, a mighty denial of our individual presumption. Sentiment shuffles along and stubbornly opposes its dramaturgy and its antiquity to all prophecies. Moderns are stupefied to find that love is not always lovable, that it does not coincide with justice or equality, that it is a feudal, antidemocratic passion. By granting it autonomy, we have let the genie out of the bottle, but the beverage is bittersweet.

What have we ultimately gained through this liberation? The right be alone! And that is not a small advance if we consider that the church long condemned *autarky* (being self-sufficient, not needing anyone) as a proof of pride, and that the nineteenth century consigned celibacy, with its odor of onanism and poverty, to opprobrium. In France, there are 14 million unmarried people, 170 million in the European Union as a whole, and that is not an accident. Being unmarried no longer means living alone or without children, and unmarried persons often have richer personal relationships than married ones. It remains that this is a negative victory, by the simple fact that it is not directed or controlled by someone else.

The Two Hypocrisies

If passionate love is, in various forms, part of all civilizations, from Arab-Andalusian mystical poetry to the great literatures of Persia, China, Japan, and India, what is peculiarly Western, from Plato's *Symposium* and the Christian gospels to modern liberators, is the will to assign a political or spiritual purpose to our emotional excitement. Love's lack of meaning drives most thinkers and philosophers to despair: it is absolutely necessary to find a meaning for love, whether it is called the contemplation of the Ideas (Plato), the advent of the Kingdom of God (Christians), or the completed revolution (Marxists). Consider Jean-Jacques Rousseau's *Émile*: a single man, through the power of his writing, not only reinvents pedagogy but also decrees with sovereign confidence what his hero's matrimonial life should be like, which woman suits him best, the perfect union of the sexes, the delicate balance between modesty and abandon, between submission and equality.[14] That is typical of European voluntarism: instead of starting by observing love in order to describe its development, we produce a theory that we apply to it after the fact and then are dismayed that reality adapts so badly to it.

There is an enormous gap between our practices and our discourses, between the forced euphoria we proclaim and the recognition of the rift we experience. The dominant stereotype indicates that we have succeeded, but the increasing number of books on conjugal happiness and how to achieve it suggests that it is no easier to experience than it used to be. We set rules for ourselves to which we are incapable of conforming. Here again it is Rousseau who started us down this path: the author of *Émile*, the great treatise on education of his age and the "art of training men," did not see fit to observe the principles that he decreed for others and abandoned, it seems, his five children, a common practice in an age when infantile mortality was very high. Do what I say, not what I do: a divorce between life as it is experienced and the life we would like to live that has been common since the Enlightenment.[15]

Our period deceives itself under the auspices of clear-sightedness, and our rhetoric functions to compensate for an absence. Classical hypocrisy drew an infrangible line between morals and respectability; contemporary hypocrisy draws a line between the declared ideal and the experienced reality. Hence the phariseeism, the comical ambiguities that are the common currency of our morals (and that Woody Allen's comedies reflect): we pursue a magnified image of ourselves, eager to correct our deviations and rise to the level of our Promethean ambitions.

But our hearts remain hopelessly resistant to the injunctions of their tutors. Liberation, emancipation: we only know these words. Life also consists in glorifying, and admiration is often finer than criticism. We cannot decide whether to reform love or celebrate it in all its dimensions, in all its marvelous ambivalence.

What Is an Ex?

Freud says somewhere that when we make love there are always at least six people involved because to each partner must be added the ghosts of their fathers and the mothers. In contemporary couples there are even more, because we also have to take each partner's ex-partners into account. The list sometimes looks like a record of Don Juan's conquests, a line-up of prestigious names that we tick off with voluptuous pleasure, which we brandish like medals, like those famous courtesans who collected princes, millionaires, and royalty. But it is also a record of our earlier goof-ups: an inventory of disappointed hopes, a curriculum vitae of our failures. In this respect, there is nothing worse than unlucky lovers who weep on your shoulder about their disappointments with another person. The ex has the ambiguous status of a ghost: a dead person who is not really buried, a dormant cell that can be awakened by a flare-up of love (that is why so many women conceal their lovers for fear of seeming too "loose" in the eyes of their present husbands).

There is a certain consolation in knowing that we are not the first, that our beloved has a certain experience. The adoration of which we are the object does not proceed from ignorance but from rational comparison. But we are always taking the risk, especially as we grow older, of appearing to be simply one in a long list of persons who have preceded us, a virtual family of which the absent members are sometimes legion. I, too, will be thrown like a scrap of raw meat to my successor: my manias and foibles will be discussed in detail, I will be pigeonholed, labeled—case closed. This is the lover's naïve dream: to erase all predecessors, to relegate them to the status of rough drafts of which he is the final version. But love does not correspond to the notion of progress, the last one does not recapitulate all the others: there are youthful romances that seem to be summits of perfection in happiness and sensorial plenitude, after which everything else seems to be only tedious repetition, mediocrity.

The ex can dampen our enthusiasm by inappropriate revelations, for example by suggesting that with the beloved we are engaging in repetition pure and simple: the same formulas, the same attentions, the same audacities. We have just refilled a slot that pre-existed us. It is worse yet when we learn that he or she has practiced sublime deprivations with others that are denied us. The ex looks at us mockingly like someone who knows the music and seems to be saying to us: you'll fail just as I did, but go ahead and try anyway. We would so much like to prove to him that he is mistaken about the person in question, that he has failed to see her, to cherish her as she deserves.

Today most of us live in a serial polygamy (or a serial monogamy); our love-lives are governed by the principle of addition. There was John, and then Paul, and then Serge, or

Aline, and Diane, and Rachel—and we could go on to list all the saints in the calendar. Some people have accumulated so many love affairs in the course of their lives that statistics could be based on them.

Ultimately, we feel an unfathomable gratitude to this group of men and women whom we have cherished, scarred, wounded, and failed to love as we should: they have made us what we are and a bit of their substance remains in our flesh right up to the end. ■

CHAPTER 2

Seduction as a Market

Every person shines with a false splendor in the eyes
of someone else; everyone is envied while he himself
is envious.

BERNARD LE BOVIER DE FONTENELLE

I was so shy that I always managed somehow to
commit the fault I was most anxious to avoid.

VLADIMIR NABOKOV, *The Real Life
of Sebastian Knight*

The Intoxication of the Diverse

We begin our careers in love without keys or rules, with bits
of information picked up here and there. We don't know
the codes of this fabulous universe, and even if we eventually manage to learn them, they immediately change.
This period in life (which sometimes continues a very long
time) we call adolescence, during which we are dazzled by
the beauty of other beings and amazed at our awkwardness
in approaching them. For anyone who is not spoiled by
the spirit of sorrow, the world is red-hot, a place of endless

charms. There is no way to contradict the marvelous faces that taunt us: there are more of them on Earth than I'll ever be able to possess, there are too many to embrace, to desire. Supply exceeds demand. Large cities are precisely such places of human density that suggest a more ardent life. In them, love is not the same as it is in suburbia or the countryside: in the latter a slow pace, few pals, petty intrigues; in the former, an abundance of possible partners, the collision of appetites, the transgression of class barriers, the enigmatic reign of people we do not know.

Adolescence is also the inability to choose, a gluttonous age in which drives take precedence over reason and we find people equally seductive because they incarnate the splendor of the multiple. Young men and women are wonderful because they are seen as a group: each one, far from eclipsing the others, magnifies them. An intoxication with the countless pleasures that hover over every gathering, a flare-up of desires, a constant provocation. Proust somewhere speaks, regarding young women on a beach, of "that vague desire to love that hesitates to choose among them all," each one being simultaneously unique and just one hue among others in the group. Before loving one particular person, we enjoy the diversity of humans in the street, in public places. The beloved will be shadowed by this multitude sacrificed to her advantage, and which she will have to supplant—a formidable task. Mystics use the term *explesis* to refer to this aesthetic delight in the manifestations of the divine. Similarly, there is a sacred thrill, an astonishment of persons who seek each other, admire each other, and never tire of looking at each other.

Not for You

The liberation of our mores bore within itself a great promise: that of a banquet open to everyone. But our careers in love also begin with the experience of rejection. We pay for our wonder by being turned down flat: our eyes call for urgent embraces that no contact confirms. The great cities tell us: everything is possible. Then why does little or nothing happen to me? Before enduring any specific sorrow, the subject in love experiences his own invisibility. In a free world, obstacles to desire are legion because they are subject to the strictest subjectivity: the old society of social orders decreed codes for pairing people up, and the prohibitions concerned money and class. The art of courting involved learning social norms, politeness, appropriate behavior, generosity. Now a tiny detail can turn against us or help us: our age, size, looks, dress, or voice. Inclinations and disinclinations are all the stronger because they are arbitrary. Who has not experienced these abrupt reversals in which we pass from pleasure to revulsion because of a detail, a facial expression, a way of laughing? And just as love can be born in an instant, so can a hatred in which we are consumed by a total aversion to someone whose only fault is that she exists. The poisonous specter of rejection haunts our slightest affections. Do not touch: this sign in museums and shops also sums up a crucial experience for all of us.

For love, there is one appropriate word, no matter how problematic it is: *market*. The coded exchange of partners may have always preceded the exchange of goods. In this human commerce, each person has a grade that varies depending on the day, social position, or fortune. The fortunate are followed by a cortege of suitors, the disadvantaged by a mass of fiascoes. Except for those favored individuals who parade about in their luminous aura, the market in male and female charm is subject to laws that are all the more implacable because they are tacit and recognized by everyone. We are involved in this war of appearances. To observe is to evaluate and thus to reject. Rejection is so terrible in democratic countries because it cannot be blamed on the wickedness of the state or ukases issued by a church. If I am not received with open arms, I have only myself to blame; I may be dying of desire, but it is my being as such that leaves the other person cold. The judgment is as final as one handed down by a court: no thanks, not you.

Has it been pointed out that the myth of Prince Charming is both a masculine and a feminine dream (just as there is penis envy among girls and vagina envy among boys)? What little human has not secretly dreamed of escaping the platitude of his life to awaken transfigured, radiant with charm? Traditionally, only males, who are supposed to take the first steps, are exposed to the perils of vexation, and the ridiculous suitor has become a literary archetype. Now women, proud of their recent liberation, can take the initiative and be rejected in their turn, running the risk of getting bogged down in the same awkwardness. There are no more Don Juans since there have been Doña Juanas, but there are many boys who are upset about this role reversal, whereas they ought to be delighted by it. The drama of old-fashioned seduction involved three characters: the community, mores, and woman. In a single gesture, one had to appease the first, respect the second, and attract the third. One had to say "I love you" instead of "I want you" and obey the codes in force the better to arrive at one's ends. The drama of contemporary seduction involves two individuals who risk their lives in this enterprise. To go toward the other is to become an object, because the object can make me suffer, and it takes a great deal of tact to say no without wounding.

How is it possible to be like Emma Bovary, George Steiner asked, in a world in which all desires are realizable? Because they are not and never will be. Our society, which constantly praises the radiant power of pleasure, penalizes more than ever those who are excluded from it, those who have been denied the right to pleasure. Dissatisfaction is all the greater because hedonism has been imposed as the norm. The market in frustration is organized in such a way as to retail charm and boldness in the form of advice, care, and gadgets. Our "liberated" era makes the fate of solitary people all the more bitter, as effaced individuals relegated to their anonymity when everyone is supposed to be enjoying pleasure. Alison Lurie says somewhere that ugly women get laid much more often than we imagine, but they have to listen to their lovers' complaints about the sufferings inflicted on them by beautiful women. There is a terrible irony in liberation: men and women, who are both victims and accomplices, persecute one another in the name of youth, health, physical beauty. Everything that was once an instrument of liberation has now become an instrument of enslavement as well.

Disenchantment and Surprise

"There are two catastrophes in life," George Bernard Shaw said, "when our desires are satisfied and when they are not." According to him, we constantly oscillate between hope and disappointment, the latter growing out of hope fulfilled. A whole school of thought emphasizes the beauty of anticipation at the expense of realization. "Only that which does not exist is beautiful," Rousseau said, underlining the role of the imagination in amorous encounters (*Émile*, p. 871). "Independently of what happens or doesn't happen, only the waiting is magnificent," André Breton wrote in turn. Illusion supplants the real and life moves from the heroic dreams of youth to the disillusionment of adulthood. "The best part of love," Clemenceau is supposed to have said, "is when you're going up the stairs": a sinister view that is redolent of furnished rooms, cheap love affairs on the side, and furtive rendezvous from five to seven.

To this Romantic cliché we can oppose another experience: that of the happy surprise when the event turns out to be richer than we had expected. Between dreaming one's life and dreaming one's dreams there is a third term: living a life that takes our breath away by its superabundance and emphasizes the poverty of our dreams. "I call the mind's intoxication," said Ruysbroek, a Flemish mystic of the Renaissance, "that state in which pleasure exceeds the possibilities that desire had glimpsed." Answered prayers are insipid as soon as our wishes have been fulfilled—that is, killed. Every exhilarating love surpasses in opulence and fervor what we expected of it: something occurs that is different from what we wanted, and then our breath is literally taken away. Lost illusions are also the path that leads to a miracle: marvelous disappointment. ∎

A Sorting Machine

Seduction, like grace in Calvinism, is a sorting machine. In the most common learning experience in the world, I learn that I am not always desired by those I desire, loved by those I love, and that I enter this universe as a potential reject. A wallflower: the range of this expression is not limited to ballrooms and parties. Some people are wallflowers all their lives, while others are adored from the start and don't know how to deal with all their admirers. The miracle of being preferred: a favor that fulfills us and excludes everyone else. Being attractive is as inexplicable as being unattractive: why do some people follow us around while others hardly deign to look at us? (Sade resolved the problem in his own way: everyone who attracts us has an obligation to grant us his favors immediately, just as we have an obligation to grant ours to those who desire us. For him, desire was a debt, while for Fourier it was a gift that attractive people agree to grant the rest of humanity.)

The success enjoyed by a writer like Michel Houellebecq, with his combination of black humor and pessimism, can be explained in this way: he has created a sort of international federation of losers in love, and revealed the lie of hedonism, which is one form of feudalism among others. He has provided a voice for those without a voice, just as Woody Allen had done in his early films that show the unattractive taking revenge on playboys. Contrary to a boastful expression, in love we cannot "have whomever we want," but only whomever we can or whoever is willing to have us. When the two coincide, it is a miracle. But "everything precious is as difficult as it is rare" (Spinoza). Some people think themselves irresistible and are convinced that they have mobs of admirers following them around, so that they interpret your refusal as an error of judgment, almost a lack of taste.

Consider exclusive clubs and night clubs: selecting their clientele on the basis of notoriety or youth, they are temples of the stock market in bodies, directly governed by the laws of competition against the background of deafening music and affected laughter. People go there to see and be seen, and judgments are made on the basis of a single glance. In theory, all that matters is having fun, enjoying oneself, and the gathering together of hundreds of individuals bound together by rhythm and movement. But clubs also control the modes of encounter, if only by the decibel level, which makes conversation difficult. There is little kindness in these pleasure palaces, which are for many people places of torment, and resemble personnel offices in large companies. (That is also the spirit of "speed dating," in which you have seven minutes to make yourself interesting.) A world of pure artifice, instantaneous infatuation: youth is displayed as a spectacle for itself, devotes itself to the adoration of perishable things. A hallucinatory vision of certain creatures whom we watch dancing the way we would look upon the impossible. Total glories of the flesh, absolute enchantment. The magnates display themselves before the plebeians who applaud them and ask for more. A universe that owes nothing to intelligence or merit but only to flashiness, affluence, and showing-off: you are what you seem to be, nothing more. Everyone is supposed to have fun amid Dionysian crowds, but the bids are so high that they often look more like punishments. In this great fair of narcissisms, some people get excessive exposure because others, who are in the majority, applaud them.

It is in the name of liberated desire, which has been freed from the prisons in which priests and morality had confined it, that the most profound forms of segregation take place. To desire is first of all to exclude, to measure faces and bodies by the standards of the code of stereotyped beauty. An individual's talent then consists entirely in discovering a way to circumvent the laws of this selection, to find, as the French say, a shoe that fits his foot. It is a miracle that in the end even the least favored are able to find someone and to penetrate the immense wall that bars their access to others. More intriguing than the classical attraction to beauty is the incomprehensible attraction to ordinary creatures. That unattractive, even very ugly men or women arouse intense feelings, mad transports of passion—that is the real miracle.[1]

The Revenge of the Eclipsed

Some people have made seduction a way of life. Incapable of resisting opportunities, they give priority to the nascent state; they are collectors of beginnings. They become infatuated with unknown persons whom they leave as soon as another appears on the horizon. For them, the amorous sequence is short: the end almost coincides with the beginning; excitation has to be followed by execution, presto. What is a man-eater? A skirt-chaser? People who like digressions. They prefer the hunt to the capture, sensation to emotion: certain romantic places call imperatively for an affair, it matters little with whom. They are equally moved by an ugly woman or a fat man: they care little about the appearances because the only thing that matters is the shock of the new. How long it lasts or what kind of exchange is involved does not interest them; they find their joy in furtive contact, the whirlwind of rendezvous. Although they generally settle down before they're fifty, they have the feeling, justified or not, that they have lived better than most people. They like the perfume of love more than people, they are happy buccaneers who exhibit their trophies to attract others. Their calculated nonchalance protects them: no affront knocks them out of the saddle, they merely attack again. Whereas the lover stammers, the seducer swaggers: he shows off his skill, his gold and scarlet, and goes straight for his target, infallible. (The male cruiser is the plebeian version of the worldly charmer; preferring slaughter to subtlety, he endures endless snubs and has a tried and true line from which he never deviates. As they age, the sidewalk seducer and the pleasure-seeker with a face-lift sink into the same pathetic repetition of worn-out, threadbare recipes.)

Anyone who lacks this skill mourns missed opportunities: what might have happened but didn't—the word that was not uttered, the gesture that was not made. Cruising for sexual partners leads to aggression; you speak to a stranger in a public place, you accost him or her (*accosting* was originally a pirates' term). But if you find someone attractive, how can you get her attention without accosting her? This kind of question can take a lifetime to answer. There are now coaches to teach you the delicate art of approaching a desired person, the witty remarks that never fail to bring a smile to the most severe of faces. As it always has, desire requires us to dissimulate: if we no longer say "I love you" straight out, neither do we tell a woman that we just want her luscious breasts, her ample ass. We have to equivocate.

An impossible equation: the more I am seduced, the less I succeed in seducing; I am petrified by inhibition. In a very high-tension climate, I should be amusing, brilliant, thoroughly relaxed. Totally flummoxed, I am struck dumb, dulled by my desire to be inventive. To court someone is first of all to blow one's own trumpet, to engage in self-embellishment. Even the most paralyzed lover has to pretend to be a lady-killer, to make use of the stratagems of flashiness. The adoring lover used to be a strutting beau who was able to shine and yield to the excitement of bidding at the risk of falling into virtuosity. But there is also a seductiveness in the refusal to seduce. There are strategies of silence and simplicity that captivate more than gratuitous volubility. Not to mention the figure of the charming, dazed lover who wins hearts by making one blunder after another. The really fine encounter is one that is unexpected and unaware of its value, and thus escapes the obligation to produce a result. If something happens, it is like the denouement of a story that was not premeditated. The obligation to proceed with verve is suspended for a freewheeling conversation that develops at its own pace because there is nothing at stake. A divine stroke of luck has held out a helping hand: it is up to us to seize it or forget it.

There is nothing more beautiful than the stubbornness of two people who have exchanged a look in a bus or on a train and want at any price to see each other again and put classified ads in the newspapers. (The personals in the Paris newspaper *Libération* are the quintessence of contemporary romance.) It is on the Internet that these bypassing strategies are flourishing: people try their luck with kindred souls, concealing themselves at first if necessary and misrepresenting themselves with their photos. Thus the terror of the preliminaries is avoided: for those who don't dare approach girls in the street or declare their love to a stranger, there remains the second chance on the computer screen. Sometimes people remain skeptical faced by these encyclopedias of lonely hearts calling out for help. But here there are no intermediaries: the websites bring together consenting adults who develop relationships in accord with their affinities and desires. These sites are vast sorting centers that pair up masses of people, whereas matrimonial agencies are small provincial operations run by supervisors who know their clientele. In them, seducers have multiple flings, and sentimentalists seek a lasting relationship. Every day, many thousands of agreements are made and unmade. The Internet is a formidable accelerator: every whim, even the most ludicrous, finds its home there. Many people are more interested in searching than in finding: they are dazzled by the number of possible adventures and wander like sultans through this virtual harem and only seldom if ever give their appetites material form.

Especially because cybernauts can disappear with a click of their mouse: the other is at my disposition, whenever I want. On websites like Meetic, Match.com, and Netclub, people construct themselves as ideal partners, smoothing out all their asperities, and offering their best profile. One shops among the candidates but is oneself part of the market. The same people who complain loudly about violations of privacy display themselves in their blogs, exhibiting themselves in daring positions: the desire for recognition wins out over the concern for prudence. Whence the delightful mix-ups that take place on the Internet, very much in the tradition of libertine novels, where a wife tracks down her husband and sets up a rendezvous with him, passing herself off as a mysterious stranger. Computerized browsing does not evade encounters, it delays them, prepares them under the best auspices. The same implacable laws will be in force as soon as the persons involved are in contact. Unless the filter of the computer screen sanctions a phobia about contact. The philosopher of science Dominique Lecourt has coined a nice neologism, *cyberia*, to designate the Web addicts who let themselves be caught in the great universal net in order to escape their contemporaries.

Every shy person thus nourishes two contradictory dreams: that of an immediate accord of epidermises and that of an instantaneous communion of souls. The dream of a desire that is not ostracized, in which bodies achieve sensual pleasure without examination: homosexual cruising, back rooms, and swingers' clubs incarnate this communism of pleasure in which no one is supposed to be excluded from the banquet of the flesh. And the opposite dream of a transparency of hearts, of a consonance of minds that avoids superfluous chit-chat and allows one to enter into symbiosis with the chosen person, beyond all the liturgies of gallantry. Neither of these two procedures could be raised to the rank of a solution: the fluidity of exchanges is still limited by the density of individuals. There will always be men and women before whom we remain speechless. Hence we long for the security of home, where we don't have to prove anything, where in theory we are not subject to constant evaluation. But even the most ovine conjugal life needs movement, and the couple—like the nation, according to Renan—is a daily plebiscite. No one is excused from the duty of having to please, even after twenty years of marriage. There is no place beyond seduction.

What Do We Call Consent?

By a strange reversal, almost half a century after May 1968, the notion of consent has come under suspicion. Many people now see in it the symptom of an imposed servitude[2] and condemn a general manipulation in all the ways in which the scene of love is staged. A sly return of the old cultural pessimism that decreed that human beings were too immature to deserve freedom. The verb *to consent* has two meanings: to accept and to desire. To say "I am willing" or "I really want" is not the same thing. A factual situation that is tolerable on the one hand, an intense wish on the other. We can resign ourselves to a poorly paid job, because it is better than nothing and because we have to eat. Shall we then say that workers and employees do not consent to their condition? No, but they do so with reservations and the hope of improving it someday: their *yes* is a *yes, maybe* that does not exclude a possible disappointment or an eventual refusal. To cast doubt on every form of approbation is to depict human beings as always captive, subjugated.

We understand what is at stake in this debate: a twofold conception of freedom as sovereignty and as "knowledge of necessity" (Spinoza). In one case, we are never free because we are never omnipotent, and we remain under influence even in our most private decisions. Human relations are seen as masked forms of violence. In the other case, inversely, we can emphasize that we always give our consent in a certain ignorance of our own desire, in a chiaroscuro

of desire and reticence, and that our will must compromise
with adversity the better to get around it. Neither absolute independence nor total enslavement are suitable for
describing the human condition, which is constituted by
everyone's ability to escape a code, a social origin, a nature.
And still more by the ability to make mistakes and to rectify
them.

If everything in human interaction is a power relationship, everything is a constraint, and we are living in a perpetual Hell. But this kind of criticism is not exempt from an
internal contradiction: people are supposed to be in chains,
with the exception of the few people who see things clearly
and condemn the masquerade. How have they managed to
escape the general conditioning? We may wonder whether
this exercise of lucidity is not the height of condescension:
to the paternalism of the person who decrees that some of
his contemporaries are slaves and at the same time infan-
tilizes them is added the blindness of the accuser who dis-
trusts everything except his own distrust. He thinks he has
penetrated the most secret mysteries of the human heart,
but he has only set his own naïveté to music.   ■

The Desire Police

Certain feminist movements, especially in North America,
have been trying for the past forty years to criminalize
cruising for sex or at least to restrict it. In offices and in
companies, and in the university as well, we see the rise
of dress codes (women are asked not to wear revealing or
form-fitting clothing), speech codes (every compliment,
every prolonged look, every intrusive commentary is seen
as incipient harassment) that give relations between the
sexes a certain rigidity. Whence the stereotypical scene in

American films: a pressure cooker about to blow up. A man and a woman who work together for professional reasons realize that they are attracted to each other. They redouble their efforts to treat each other coolly, and even insult one another, until an accidental touch leads them to the fatal act: they hungrily embrace, have sex, panting heavily, then throw their clothes back on. The return of the repressed: here sexuality is combined with an epileptic fit.[3] Reiterated in every tone, the same scene becomes ridiculous and makes us long for the old films in which people yielded with a certain elegance. The subtext of these narrative fillers: sexuality is an irresistible drive that has to be satisfied so that one doesn't have to think about it anymore. Whereas the Frenchman says: "Faisons l'amour," the American in television series and films says: "Let's have sex." The difference is not merely semantic, it reflects two worldviews: in the latter case it is a matter of a pressing, animal need, like hunger or thirst, and in the former of a complex act that gives rise to a whole erotics, love that makes us as much as we make it, a subtle construction rather than a physical evacuation. Ceremony on the one hand, bestiality on the other.

In English-speaking universities, every conversation with a student, male or female, has to be either recorded on tape or conducted in a room with an open door. The slightest approach can give rise to a complaint. Any sexual relationship between a professor and a student, even if the latter is of age and consenting, can result in the professor's dismissal.[4] In business, management reserves the right to meddle in private exchanges if the terms employed are considered scabrous or degrading, of a nature likely to lead to a hostile environment! Resort is made to specialized seminars, to "love contracts" between employees who want to get involved and agree not to sue the company in the event that the relationship ends. It may be recalled that in the early 1990s, a university in Ohio promulgated, unsuccessfully, a charter regulating private sexual acts between students: the latter were supposed to report in writing and in full detail every stage (touching the breasts, taking off the blouse, etc.) and submit this program to the responsible official. Some people in a France that now recognizes the crime of sexual harassment in the workplace, the abuse of a position of power, would like to extend it to all human relations and criminalize mistakes, suggestions, insinuations. But for the moment, France is resisting this climate of moral McCarthyism.

It is true that violence against women increases as their independence increases: there is a danger that we will even see an unprecedented explosion of violence to punish them for having raised their heads. Some men's resentment of them is comparable to the rage of a slaveholder reacting to the abolition of slavery. Progress in liberating women goes hand in hand with hatred of liberated women. It would be absurd to deduce from this that seduction will be prohibited; seduction persists, fortunately, and even in accord with what women want. It also participates in the great egalitarian process, because it has to substitute persuasion for authority, and because in seducing someone has to seek her consent instead of forcing her. One of my students at Sciences-Po, a lovely girl of Japanese origin from Quebec, told us in public about her disappointment with North American men, whose enthusiasm was paralyzed by sexual correctness. She spent her vacations in Italy in order to be more openly approached by boys; she had sufficient self-confidence to get rid of the unwelcome ones. Whereas in the United States the coexistence of the sexes always seems on the verge of exploding, Europe is better protected against this plague by the age-old culture of gallantry. This etiquette, which may be heir to the "erotics of the troubadours" (René Nelli) that wove a whole ritual of allegiance and submission between a knight and his lady, is a way of reintroducing aristocratic manners within democratic leveling. It is not only a preparation for courtesy, but also converts animal desire to attention and delicacy, civilizes it on the basis of its impurities. It shapes both sexes' common taste for conversation, exchange, and wit that gives their discussions depth and vivacity. (The French spirit, Montesquieu said, is the art of speaking seriously about frivolous things and frivolously about serious things.) It is the pleasure we take in pleasing, in playing with the other, in duping the other with our approval—unless it is the other who is leading us by the nose. Even if we skip steps, the forms have to be observed; for example, we have to respect the transition from the formal *vous* to the intimate *tu*, which remains, in many languages, an obligatory marker. The ambiguous status of the compliment: depreciated in the eighteenth century as aping the courtier, suspected by some activists in the 1960s, it may, if it is well formulated, be received as tribute that confirms us in our self-esteem. The finest compliments are the most disinterested ones that are made by people who are anonymous or of our same sex. To challenge the mask, the chiaroscuro, to impose all at once the limpidity of hearts and of bodies, is to do away with the fertile trials that nascent love needs in order to develop.

Ruses and schemes better promote the cause of sentiments than a dreary clarity.

The Defeat of the Phantasm

A fundamental question: do we really choose our partners, or are we in fact programmed when we think we are acting with full lucidity? Two discourses cast doubt on the gratuity of our inclinations: sociology sees in them the confirmation of a class causality, whereas psychoanalysis sees in them the symptom of unresolved tensions with our parents.[5] Although we can analyze our options at great length, in the end we always have to choose, even within a certain framework, this person rather than that, without outside intervention. Our decisions are autonomous in relation to our individual or social conditioning. It may even happen that we surprise ourselves by choosing unexpected partners very distant from our culture or milieu. More interesting than this Byzantine question, however, is that of *a posteriori* predestination: freedom invents a determinism for itself after the fact. The lovers cannot not have met, they were meant for each other even before they met. They convert to fate the chance that brought them together at a certain time and place: it is inconceivable that this encounter might not have occurred. Anything rather than that terrible suspicion: if it hadn't been you, it would have been someone else! Among the dozens of people considered, the beloved face must have stood out from all others. Him (or her) and no one else: ecstasy and trembling.

There are people so moved by others' desire for them that they yield less because they are inclined to do so than because they want to respond to the homage paid them. As we get older, we may acquire quite different tastes, become less attracted by the standard aesthetic baubles and go instead for the most diverse human types: preferring charm to beauty, sexiness to sweetness, the captivating anomaly to dull majesty. Love worships ravishing little imperfections, heart-rending defects that move us more than a perfect body. We mustn't censure our predilections but rather enrich them, multiply them. They root us in the real as much as they limit us; love is also the defeat of the phantasm, of purely plastic attributes. We can enrich ourselves with men or women who are not "our kind," broaden the spectrum of our references. Consider for example this odd exchange: at a time when Europeans, Australians, and North Americans want to look tanned, and endanger themselves by excessive exposure to the sun, Africans, Chinese, and Filipinos dream of lightening their skins at the risk of destroying their pigmentation and incurring irreparable damage. A predominance of colonial prejudices, the influence of the American model? That is far from clear. Rather the fact that every part of the world dreams of being the other one, light-skinned people want to be dark-skinned, the tanned want to have pale faces. Everything that runs counter to the dominant opinion, everything that reverses the order of generations and conditions—the beautiful woman with the ugly man, the homely woman with the handsome man, the young man with mature woman, the girl with the graybeard, the poor with the rich—must be celebrated.

Let us not dream of putting an end to the tyranny of beauty, let us dream of disturbing it, of seeing in accord with several contradictory norms at the same time. After all, fashion exists not to impose models on us but to reassure us, to tell us how to dress, how to make ourselves up. It is a calming factor: before standardizing us, it helps us out. Of course, seduction is also a career for a certain number of people, whose only assets are their faces and their anatomies. And who can blame them? How can one make a career out of one's beauty when one is a married, middle-class lady, Balzac asked in *Cousin Bette*.[6] He recommended a fortunate concatenation of circumstances, a large city full of idle people and millionaires, a great deal of elegance and wit, a total absence of scruples, and especially a husband who turns a blind eye. Previously reserved for women, this status has been open to men ever since Maupassant's "Bel Ami," who climbs all the rungs of society thanks to his talents as a seducer of women. (In French, gigolos are called "beavers" [*castors*], after an animal that constructs its house with its tail.) How many positions in the upper spheres of politics, the economy, and culture have been acquired by means of personal qualities as much as by going to bed with one's superiors?

Even if it is diverted for the purposes of ambition, seduction maintains a climate of complicity between men and women, gives priority to bonds over separation, attraction over silence. In the end, nothing is out of style: neither old-fashioned courting nor brief encounters nor brusque abductions nor love at first sight: extreme sophistication combined with extreme crudeness. The rules have changed, but the old rules are still in force. It is the superimposition of the two that explains our current disorientation. Everything is obsolete, everything remains pertinent. Our mores have not constructed a new house for themselves: this one bears a strange resemblance to the old one, even if license seems more prominent and the circulation of couples more rapid. A psychological train wreck for contemporary people inhabited by multiple customs and traditions.

If we want to understand contemporary mores in the Western world, we have to rely not on the concept of succession but rather on that of superimposition. Our ambition is recapitulative, our model is cumulative, simultaneously Romantic and libertine, altruistic and capricious, courtly and pornographic, an immense echo chamber in which the most accepted practices and the strangest ones coexist side by side. Like Rome—in which Freud saw the palimpsest-city par excellence, where all centuries overlap, from the Roman republic to the Renaissance—the sentiment of love does not recognize divisions of time, and makes us the contemporaries of distant ages. That is the temporal system of our affections, multilayered, simultaneously very much in advance and very archaic, a vast range of passions that can be run through at will. Thus it is pointless to expect our contradictions to some day be resolved in a better society. They will continue to coexist forever, even if there may be partial improvements, occasional clear spells. We have to give up trying to save sentiment from itself, to find a way out of our affective chaos.

Separation, an Art of Finesse

Modern separation irresistibly reminds us of dismissal procedures in business. A delicate moment for both parties, because the goal is to lance the abscess without making a mess, to "cut the fat" without producing a tragedy. The other has to accept his disgrace, not moan and weep. The things we are prepared to do to get rid of someone who is a burden, the heights of cowardice and bad faith we attain, the pathetic ruses we invent to soften the blow! The gentleness with which we give him the bad news barely conceals our desire to see him decamp immediately. If he protests, we know how to make him solely responsible for his misfortune. He had been warned! To banishment is added the additional degradation of being at fault. The truth smacks him in the face as it does on the last page of a detective novel, and he is the culprit to boot! The culminating lack of consideration: dismissing the other by text message, like a common trader!

There are cases, inventoried by the best authors (Benjamin Constant, Marcel Proust), in which separation triggers love instead of putting an end to it. "Such is the strangeness of our miserable hearts that leaving those whose company gave us no pleasure causes us great pain" (*Adolphe*). The partner has to leave for us to finally love her: breaking off the relationship revives what living side by side had anesthetized, and the absent person becomes marvelous by the simple fact that she is no longer there. A variant: showing no reaction to the fatal announcement, letting oneself be dismissed without saying a word. The lover hoped for supplications, pleas, and then you go out the door without batting an eye. A horrible suspicion: I'm leaving him, and he doesn't care, maybe down deep he even wanted this. An elegant way of making the break: letting the other take the initiative when you've preceded her on the path to separation. You push her to make the break so you don't have to do it. Being left is often better than leaving oneself, it avoids the burden of remorse. Inversely, many men and women take the initiative in breaking off for fear of being left for someone younger. They refuse to be replaced, and to forestall catastrophe they trigger it right away, even though they will suffer enormously.

There are two stages in this trajectory of love: the one in which freedom desires its own abolition and makes, in fear and convulsion, the leap into the other, and the one in which, disappointed, it returns to itself as from an illusion, a sort of intoxication. Then "I want my freedom back" means: I prefer sobering up to imprisonment, I want to escape from the spell. This disenchantment is often a sad conquest, and as soon as they have left a relationship most people start dreaming about another delicious yoke that will deprive them of their freedom. Starting over with someone else, repeating the same mistakes, repeating better. Separating from someone means leaving behind all the worlds that he incarnated. And when he is gone, the universes he initiated continue to gravitate around us like so many phantoms.

Ultimately, leaving is more difficult than beginning: we hesitate to leave someone whom we think we no longer love but who assures our comfort and security. Someone who leaves us sometimes does us a favor, forces us to get a grip on ourselves: the horror of those couples who cling to one another like two tapeworms and grow thin because they dare not separate. In the United States as in Europe, divorce counselors organize ceremonies in which the wedding ring is buried, the wedding gown thrown in the fire. The classic divorce, with its dramaturgy, its mutual letters of accusation, made those involved detest one another: people wanted to make it less dramatic, to see the failure positively, to open a new era. Now you're free again, we tell the weeping, ravaged wife who has been thrown over for a snip of a girl at least ten years younger, rejoice! But no separation is easy or amounts to just making a new start: former partners echo inside us long after they have left, come back to haunt us, tug at our sleeves. Love sometimes flares up fifteen or twenty years later for people we met in our youth when we were unable to appreciate them. Finally, there are couples who continue to coexist in the mind even after they have ceased seeing each other. A breakup is the way their love has chosen to prolong itself without the problems of living together. ∎

CHAPTER 3

I Love You: Weakness and Capture

To say to someone: I love you, is to tell him:
You shall not die.

GABRIEL MARCEL

There are people who would never have fallen in love
had they never heard people talk about love.

FRANÇOIS DE LA ROCHEFOUCAULD

I tell a woman that I love her. . . . Have I not simply
promised . . . that this word will have the meaning
we give it by living together? We are going to create
it, and that is a great task. Has it waited for us to give
it the meaning that we shall give it? And if our goal is
to give it a meaning, that is because we are going to
work for it, not for us, and thus it is our master.

BRICE PARRAIN, *Recherches sur le langage*

We know the famous scene in Molière where the "bourgeois
gentleman" is learning rhetoric, an art dear to the *Précieuses*
of his time, and repeats with delight, turning it this way
and that, the sentence: "Marquise, vos beaux yeux me font
mourir d'amour." Even when the sentence is reversed, it

continues to make sense. In that period, gallantry as an aristocratic code combined three latent defects: obscurity, pretense, and ridiculousness. Eighteenth-century philosophers, and Rousseau first of all, did not fail to subject it to criticism and to oppose to it the imperative of authenticity. However, they failed to imagine that in its very excesses it might sometimes be sincere.

Similarly, the language of love is wholly borrowed, in both senses of the term: affected and anterior to us. Words that have been repeated thousands of times to express a single sentiment; however, this does not mean that the sentiment is false, but only that it uses a collective vehicle for a personal end. Love is first of all a rumor that whispers in our ears the most beautiful promises: we venerate it before we experience it in actuality, we rehearse this play for years without understanding it. Far from being a spontaneous feeling, it is inculcated in us as a code by our family and by society. From an early age, we have access to a treasury of loving words that we apply to those close to us, to pets, and to babies. Expressions that are ludicrous and touching, they preexist us and combine affection with an automatic character: my angel, my dear, are neither you nor I, but everyone and anyone at all. Not to mention that we often love in a similar way people who are different, playing out almost exactly the same scenario with them. *I love you*: the most intimate in the grip of the most anonymous, the first time as a repetition of a very ancient litany. I would have to create unique words that are valid only in the instant that I utter them and then disintegrate. But the road I invent with the beloved has to start from paths beaten by millions of others before me.

The Impossible Coincidence

I love you can be understood as a plea, a contract, a seizure, a debt. This formula that burns my lips is useful first of all for acknowledging emotional excitement. I celebrate the feverishness that the other arouses in me and protest against the disorder into which it plunges me. By his very presence, a stranger has broken my life into two parts, and I would like to return to myself without losing him. The collision of love is the irruption of a verticality in the boring calm of life: it is pain and pleasure, destabilizing and reenergizing, a burning and a fragrance. How to tame this other who overpowers me, strikes me like a thunderbolt from on high? By an admission that is both a supplication and an interrogation.

Beneath the intoxication of *I love you* lurks the desire to capture the other and force her to respond to me. At the same time that I confess my emotional excitement, I ask a question: how about you, do you love me? If by some miracle she replies "yes," I recover my calm, I enter into the jubilation of reciprocity. *I love you* is a synchronizer: it adjusts the temporal difference between loves and puts them in the same time zone. It makes You and Me contemporaries. It is also the passport that we hold out to the other in order to enter his territory, the equivalent of a permit through which he grants us access to his universe. But the mystery resists being deflowered: everything has been said, nothing accomplished. Once the fatal sentence has been uttered, the lovers have to calibrate their existence in relation to it, show themselves worthy of it. It is difficult to retract, to go backward. We are on our way, especially since *I love you* cannot be modified by an adverb: neither "a little" nor "a lot," it is an absolute in itself that decides and rules.

I will always love you: the formula commits the one who utters it in the very moment that she says it. This "always" is another time within ordinary time: I act as if I were going to love you forever even if it is not in my power to control the variation of our feelings. The man of my life, the woman of my life: but it is one life among the multiple destinies that we traverse in the course of our lives. The oath implies confidence and a wager: by leaping over doubt and fear, it postulates that the world is a place in which we can develop together and take responsibility for ourselves. But by invoking chance, it also puts the lovers in the same insecurity, transforms them into potential murderers of one another. By confessing my emotional excitement, I become subject to a despot as capricious as he is charming, and who from one day to the next can decide to cast me back into the abyss from which he plucked me. I have entered a high-risk universe in which catastrophe can strike at any moment. Does the other stop calling me? I think I am lost. Am I calm? He dismisses me abruptly. The Italian writer Erri De Luca tells us that while he was studying at the university, he got sick. Shivering with fever, he was visited by his girlfriend, who began by warming him up and made love to him in such a magnificent way that he thought he had touched eternity. Afterward, very calmly, she told him that she was leaving him. It was not an apotheosis but an adieu.

The grammatical obviousness is misleading: With regard to the beloved I am still like peasant with regard to his lord; he retains the enormous stature from which I had tried to dislodge him. The contract of mutual servitude I had tried to establish failed, and in his presence I remain separated from him. I wanted to put him under house arrest, incarcerate him in the golden cell of our passion. But it is he who puts me in detention. The captive has become my jailer. I have not belonged to myself since I tried to appropriate him for myself. Whence the need to repeat the oath over and over. The repetition is simultaneously begging and separating. The calm doesn't last; the sweetest pledges fade after a few days and have to be reiterated ad nauseam.

Men/Women: The Rout of Clichés

Women are frivolous, sweet, sentimental, perfidious, generous, lubricious; men are cowardly, selfish, philandering, brutal, unfaithful. Besides, there are no men, they have all resigned, they are irresponsible. Never has there been such an inflation of clichés expressed by one sex about the other, each reproaching its counterpart for having changed, of having betrayed his or her stereotype without for all that canceling it. Women blame men for having become what they wanted them to be, men blame women for having changed everything while remaining the same. Formerly women were destined for the home, for the order of sentiment, men for the public sphere and for conquest; women belonged to nature, men to culture. Each sex now intends to take on the tasks assigned to the other: women work, manage, study, while fathers care for the children and in theory do their share of the housework. Do men excel in these activities? Then they are reproached for lacking authority and verve. Do their wives succeed in their professions? Then they are blamed for neglecting their children.

That is the curse of the freedoms acquired: battle exhilarates but victory disappoints, isolates, confronts us with excessive obligations. The autonomy won by women has not done away with their old responsibilities, and it has produced a overload of work. Women's loss of their preeminence for men has not led them to desert the functions that were theirs. Both men and women find themselves in the same zone of uncertainty where they have to cobble together new models on the basis of the old. They no longer understand each other, and are never where they expect to be. This mixing-up explains the nostalgia some women feel for the classical machismo that they used to abhor, while men are surprised to find themselves with female companions who are so liberated and at the same time so traditional. It is the fate of emancipation to make us disconcerting beings who float between several roles and are above all forced to construct ourselves as free individuals responsible for our acts.

The other frightens me when he moves outside his place and does not stick to any task in a permanent way. In this respect, to seek "real men" and "real women" is to seek the security of an archetype, to try to master one's dizziness. Femininity is not exhausted by the roles of mother, bluestocking, muse, or whore any more than masculinity is limited to the roles of leader, boss, and paterfamilias. Whence the same nostalgia for clarity: tell me who you are so that I know who I am. Both men and women long for the simplicity that used to preside over their divisions: they would like to put an end to indecisiveness, to confine the other in a definition. They suffer from living in an era of fluidity. If there is an identity crisis, it is common to both sexes.

Anatomy is thus no longer destiny even if it retains its prerogatives: it will never be possible for a man to procreate or have an orgasm like a woman's, nor for a woman to know the joys of an erection. If each gender reinvents the other, there is neither confusion nor rapprochement but only vacillation. The notions that they imply persist without our knowing their precise meaning. Generalities about one or the other retain a limited pertinence, but that does not make them true. Everything that one says about women—for instance, that they are tender and affective—can be said just as correctly about men: here the rule is no more than the sum of its exceptions. Some virtues and defects are equally distributed among the two sexes as a patrimony that is ultimately held in common. It is obvious that masculine and feminine ways of experiencing love are not the same, but that means that there are at least two ways of experiencing love, whatever sex the person concerned belongs to. There is no need for women to give up their femininity, or for men to give up their masculinity: in democratic countries at least, both men and women are free to invent themselves as persons even if it is still easier, even today, to be a male in our societies. Why seek desperately to reconstruct a group identity to seal off this fear?

In the name of the omnipotence of the individual, a postsexual utopia, encouraged by surgery and chemistry, would like to blur the divisions inherited from nature. Beneath the philosophical gobbledygook, it is not hard to discern the old religious mistrust of the body and of sexual differentiation, along with the otherworldly dream that runs throughout Christianity: "For at the resurrection men and women do not marry; no, they are like the angels in heaven" (Matthew 22:30). Nonetheless, it is good that humanity is divided into two parts; this bipolarity gives rise to an unexpected human richness. It would be still better if each person simultaneously confirmed and contradicted the gender to which he or she belonged and acted differently from what is expected on the basis of his or her sex. Men and women do not always speak the same language. What matters is that they continue to converse, despite misunderstandings and contradictions, without resorting to a reductive Esperanto. There have to be at least two sexes so that each dreams of the other. In my next life, I want to be born a woman. ■

Reinvent Me

The terrible enigma posed by this commandment: "Love thy neighbor as thyself." Apparently a logical absurdity: either I love myself to the detriment of others or I love the other to the detriment of myself. Therefore I would have to adore myself unreservedly in order to pour out my feelings to my neighbor! However, it is not a succession that is involved, but rather a coincidence. I love myself because others love me, tell me who I am. I need to be seen by their benevolent eyes, heard by their attentive ears.[1] They confirm me in my being, and their esteem has a germinative power.

To love oneself is to recognize a scission. Aristotle distinguished a useful egoism from a mean egoism. A fundamental discovery: to like oneself, one has to be divided. "A horse is not in disharmony with himself, therefore he is not a friend for himself." Only humans can become enemies of themselves and ultimately seek to destroy themselves. We all need the presence of others in order to put ourselves at a distance. Christianity also promotes the idea of a twofold self: worldly and divine, futile and deep, false and true. Between me and myself falls the gigantic shadow of God who has to be welcomed in by ridding oneself of everything ephemeral: a vivifying death or a mortifying life, as Francis de Sales put it. If according to Pascal the self is hateful, that is because in its thickness it presents an obstacle to the being within us that is greater than we are. To love one's neighbor as oneself is to love in her that part of eternity that we share with each other and that is the sign of our possible common redemption. Finally, Rousseau distinguished between good self-love, which is the sole guarantee of truth, and bad self-love, which has been corrupted by society.

What can we learn from these traditions? That we have to begin with self-esteem in order to forget ourselves and make room for others. Thus it is important to know oneself while one is still quite young, and then no longer think about it. Become who you are, Nietzsche said. But also become who you are not, possibly better. The Enlightenment counted on human perfectibility: we are not entirely what we are, we have reserves of intelligence, generosity, and courage that we do not suspect. Thus we are born at least twice: the second time when we create, on the basis of the self received, a liberated self, and move from the old person to the new. If psychoanalysis has one utility, it is to reconcile each person to his neurotic poverty so that he can accept himself as he is. To make peace with oneself: a misleading expression. In general, it is a matter of putting an end, not to a fierce war, but to a conflict that inhibits us and forces us to continue in the same ruts. Anyone, Freud said, who lacks narcissism lacks power, and cannot inspire confidence: thus there is a good narcissism that allows us to be our own friends while being friends to others, and there is another narcissism that betrays a fundamental doubt regarding our value, even if the borderline between the two is very slender.

Consider Simone Weil's remark: loving a stranger as one loves oneself implies as its corollary loving oneself as one loves a stranger. A perfect but inexact balance: loving oneself as another would still be according too much importance to oneself, seeing too indulgently this fascinating stranger that I am for myself. If we have to take a distance on ourselves, it is the better to disburden ourselves and approach what is far from us. Being full of ourselves prevents us from making room for others. Even someone who constantly hates herself remains riveted to herself in a tyrannical slavery. Vanity has a thousand faces, and self-flagellation is one of the most elaborate. Whence the sadness at being only for oneself, doomed to hunt one's own reflection everywhere (the success of radio and television: they create a pseudo-other who speaks to us without interlocutors, looks at us without seeing us).

To fall in love is to give things a certain relief, to embody ourselves anew in the thickness of the world, and to discover that it is richer and denser than we suspected. Love redeems us from the sin of existing: when it fails, it condemns us for the gratuitous nature of this existence. Alone, I feel myself to be simultaneously empty and saturated: if I am only myself, I am superfluous. In the abominable moment of rupture, this self that I had hoped to bracket comes back on me like a boomerang in the form of a packet of useless cares. So there I am burdened once again with a dead weight: getting up, washing, feeding myself, enduring the insanity of my interior monologue, killing time, wandering about like a lost soul. This void is overflowing. "The great, implacable amorous passions are all connected with the fact that a person imagines that he sees his most secret self behind the eyes of another" (Robert Musil). But the secret of this self is that it is entirely created by the other, by the state of exhilaration in which the other puts us: the unprecedented pleasure of being loved, that is, saved while we are still alive. Love has a germinative power, it causes something to bloom that existed only in a latent state; it frees us from the harping, impoverished ego that constitutes our personal core. It gives us back a larger, joyous ego that makes us strong and capable of great things.

The Two Kinds of Modesty

There is a natural modesty that conceals itself from others, and another modesty that blooms at the heart of erotic furor when we fail in our attempt to grasp the person who yields. We learn a body as we learn a foreign language: some people are natural polyglots, while others never get beyond an endless stammer. But the body of the beloved remains a dark continent: the way in which it gives itself to us tells us a great deal about what it dissimulates. Even at the height of passion, I feel its inviolability. Reticence persists even in the midst of lust. The obscene lies not in what is shown, but in what we will never see or possess, the combination of indecency and absence.

Nudity is first of all a test of fragility and secondarily a test of deep emotion. To undress is to make oneself vulnerable, to expose oneself to attack, to mockery. It does not suffice to take off one's clothes to trigger erotic excitement, a certain grace is required, an art that is not given to everyone. The simplest clothing is the most complex, and some stripteasers conceal more than a suit of armor would. Nudity is a creation: it arises slowly from the exchange of caresses, when a body opens up under your fingers like those Japanese paper objects that when thrown in the water expand to form a whole bouquet of flowers. The homage that another person pays to my private parts is a way of ennobling them. The tender savagery with which he treats me makes a luminous body emerge from my ordinary body. I am reborn to myself, everything that was ordinary becomes magnificent and intense.

Modesty: not the restraint that precedes love but the spasm that concludes the cycle, the ultimate form of separation. At the height of sensual pleasure, the coincidence does not occur, "the hidden does not unveil itself, the darkness is not dispersed" (Emmanuel Levinas), the communion fails.[2] Is there anything more overwhelming than the echo of orgasm on the beloved's face when it is blazing at the peak of ecstasy? Here we seem to touch the absolute, which is embodied in these convulsed features like those of the mystics who glimpsed for an instant the face of God and remained thunderstruck. What the sexual embrace resurrects is the lovers' virginity. This does not refer to little girls' hymens, which are the object of macabre speculations, but the quality of the hymen that is reborn from my caresses, endlessly recommenced. Even if I put my hands on this person, satisfy my avid desire, she remains outside my grasp, constantly rising up anew from our embraces. I have remained at the edge of the other, the eternal stranger, like Moses on the threshold of the Promised Land. ∎

The Whore Formula

There are individuals who have never doubted, from the outset, that they would be adulated, awaited.[3] It is a certitude that envelops the whole person with a radiant aura, gives him the guarantee that he is chosen. Life often sees to it that these spoiled children get their comeuppance, a correction that is all the more cruel because they thought they were invincible. Few of us enjoy such an assurance. Love produces a new *cogito*: you love me, therefore I am (Clément Rosset), I love you, therefore we are. But the being that the other confers on us by loving us is only a may-be. The formula *I love*

you can in fact become a skeleton key that facilitates everyday exchanges, as in those Hollywood films that positively
drip with tenderness among parents, infants, and spouses.
The protagonists no longer have names, they are all called
"my love, my darling," even when they are insulting each
other. There are brief *I love you*s uttered under the influence of a momentary emotion and whose validity does not
exceed the duration of the pleasurable spasm, anonymous
*I love you*s addressed to no one in particular, aggressive *I
love you*s thrown out like a packet of dirty linen, placebo *I
love you*s that are good for the person who hears them and
do no harm to the one who utters them, supplicating *I love
you*s that are requests to take complete control, narcissistic *I love you*s that merely say: I adore myself through you,
like those of a singer performing before a big crowd (what
an intense orgasm, the multitude's idolatry of him!). Not
to mention ardent proclamations followed by long periods
of silence, so that the addressee wavers between exultation
and panic. What hurts is not strangers' indifference, it is
the coolness of those close to us, or rather their intermit-
tent warmth. We think we are clasping them to our breast
and we embrace only an absence. We are rightly wary of
oaths made while embracing, just as making love prevents
us from talking about love: the tongue likes to ramble when
the flesh exults, it makes promises right and left. But the
inverse is also true: it is in the tumult of the senses that the
shy person may be able to slip in his declaration without
fearing ridicule.

    I love you: the whore's formula par excellence, which
does not mean that it is false but that it is undecidable. The
most searing secret, the most shopworn cliché. We learn

nothing from someone whom we adore except the essential point: that we are still loved. That is the only knowledge the other can give us and it is the choice between life and death. In this sense, every person who is loved is by nature fatal: it will be her and no one else, there will not be multitudes, she will remain the figure of destiny until we draw our last breath, even if she has left us.

Portrait of Turtledoves as Avengers

The declaration of love is also a blank check that we can hardly wait to cash: the marvelous gift is transformed into a debt, and we want to recoup our costs. I love you: you owe me your affection, if possible a hundred times over. Love accedes to language in the form of a financial arrangement: an account is opened in which the roles of creditor and debtor are permanently inverted. If one of the parties, upon drawing up his balance sheet, believes that he has been cheated, the equilibrium is broken. To love is first of all to subtract a person from the human community, to depopulate the world, and to ignore everything that is not him. But this sacrifice demands repayment, and if possible with interest. The chosen one has to prove to me every day that I was right to put him on a pedestal and disdain other potential suitors.

At the beginning of the eighteenth century, English moralists made an important discovery: the development of affection within families is accompanied by an increase in the number of conflicts and by a hatred that grows more intense.[4] Seeing two turtledoves, formerly so languid, transformed into ferocious warriors, going for each others' throats during a divorce proceeding, is one of the most disturbing lessons in human nature. How did they get from enthusiasm to aversion? Two temporalities are constantly superimposed in everyday life in common: the temporality of events experienced together, whether happy or difficult, and the pitiless temporality of failings that are registered in the debit column. The dynamic memory of the good years, the painful memory of grievances. The lovers sometimes act like usurers who lend their hearts on credit and ruthlessly capitalize on mistakes. Make the other pay: the expression should be taken literally. The money demanded in compensation is supposed to rectify the injury done to a narcissism that considers itself to have been duped, to have made too many sacrifices, and demands back payments due. The chest of grievances is thrown wide open: I was tricked, I gave you my best years. In a time that bans money from the domain of love, monetary requests are coming back all the more strongly because they compensate for moral injuries. Thus the prenuptial contract used in America among well-off people has at least the virtue of making things clear: by setting in advance the amount of the indemnities that the wealthier partner will pay his or her spouse in the event that they separate, it avoids mixing genres, the parasiting of the heart.[5]

Love interrogates, like a sphinx. Beneath the calm appearance, behind the smiles, it launches a constant investigation. Like police officers, lovers are following the tracks of a potential crime: they need clear signs, and don't trust any of them. They see details that no one else notices, hear things that escape the sharpest ears. A silence, a hesitation throw them into perplexity. They become detectives, spies: some have their spouses followed by a private eye, tap their computers, their cell phones, wiretap them. Statements of attachment are transformed into symptoms of betrayal, the most flagrant proofs of deception into guarantees of fidelity. Some see only treachery beneath caresses; others see only caresses beneath treachery. Suspicion as well as credulity can be sincere. The person in love suffers from a panic of interpretation and spends his time deciphering the language of the other, so familiar and at the same time so distant.

"I am not worthy of you," cries the lover in the early days. "You don't deserve me," disappointed spouses later say to each other. We declare our love as we declare war, as the proverbial expression has it, and we also open a belligerent space. A place of high intensities that can turn into high hostility. Depreciation was already inherent in the idealization, criticism in the adoration. I love you, I want you, I hate you, I'm angry at you. Exasperation is often the sentimental climate of old married people who have been feeding at the same trough and who can no longer stand each others' breath. Life in a couple then becomes a battle that two persons wage against each other in order to punish themselves for being together: under the cooing of fiancés were the rumblings of resentment, and great sentiments decline into very petty resentments.

Polite Dodges

It sometimes happens that lovers resist confessing their love, dividing up the declaration to attenuate the risks, and challenging by humor or abstention the imperative of transparency implicit in this locution. Suggesting rather than avowing, postponing the fatal revelation, not putting an end to the jurisdictional dispute. Letting love remain undeclared to avoid transforming intoxication into a transaction. However, there are few people who are wise enough to hold their tongues and engage in polite dodges: most of them want to know where they are and calm their anxiety. Invective condenses in itself the whole dramaturgy of love: capture and abandon, effusion and allergy, dizziness and law. The geometric place of the confession that disguises, the revelation that dissimulates, the truth that lies. *I love you* does not have its end in itself; it opens out onto a scene that the lovers do not even control, though they recite the first speeches. Time alone will tell if the statement was a potential act or a simple mantra to conquer the other at less risk.

Finally, there is an *I love you* of pure self-sacrifice, like that of parents for their children: a daily act of faith that is meant as a free gift. "You are a miracle of which I never tire; your existence is the best gift I have ever been given." To say that is not to subjugate the interlocutor by means of an oath, it is to free her from any obligation to us. The paradox of an offering that in no way deprives its donor but instead enriches her beyond all possession. We love our children so that someday they will abandon us; we lavish care and tenderness on them to prepare them for autonomy. We rejoice in their joy; their successes are ours; their distress wounds us personally. They do not belong to us; they owe us nothing; and they will leave us when the time comes. In the fragility of the little person, love sees its own fragility, its mortal nature: it is itself this slender spark of life that asks only to burst into flame. To love in this way is to consent, despite ourselves, to lose the other, even if that means that we will be unhappy—nothing is as sad as a family home without a family—it is to emancipate him from our grasp, to not invest him with an impossible mandate: reciprocity. "To be loved is to pass, to love is to last" (Rilke).

The Sweet Pain of Loving (Verlaine)

The French poet Louis Aragon's famous line, "Il n'y a pas d'amour heureux" ("There is no happy love") is both very beautiful and very false: it sees every relationship from the point of view of the end. The verdict has been handed down; it is inexorable and claims to be final. If the point is to let us know that we will all die someday and that humans cannot attain absolute happiness, the line simply states the obvious. If there is no happy love, how can we explain why so many people who have just escaped from a painful love affair dream of subjecting themselves to another tyrant who is both spellbinding and dangerous? The opposite claim would make more sense: there is only happy love, as long as it lasts, even if the passion eventually flickers out. Why try to besmirch and trample on what may not last; why devalue what Péguy called "the poignant grandeur of the perishable"? Two people give each other not only their bodies, pleasures, and mutual talents, but also a history unlike any other that will bind them together, even if they have to part.

The many joys of the couple: seeing love in the eyes of one's partner, having a benevolent listener, achieving great things together, daring to do together what neither would dare do alone. I am saved as soon as my beloved is at my side and witnesses my slightest act. The virtue of living in a couple: indulgence. Being accepted as I am, with my weaknesses, without being put down. A suspension of the verdict. Being able to ignore my image, whereas outside, in society, I constantly have to prove myself. It is hard to leave this cocoon of well-being to become a social animal, put on a mask, be funny, articulate. The charming possibility of being silly together, babbling and going soft in the head without being subjected to the thunderbolts of criticism, giving each other nicknames that compete with the official names.

In conjugal harmony, sentiment takes pleasure in itself, showcases itself, becomes voluble, eloquent. Life in a couple is routine, but a happy routine, a promise of security. The sweetness of familiar things, the pleasure of having the beloved at one's side every evening. Not overwhelming her with my affection, not burdening her, trying to base the greatest intimacy on the right interval. I need her at my side so that I am not constantly thinking about her and she stops troubling me by her absence.

As for the suffering involved in love, it is inseparable from felicity, our pain pleases us and we would miss it if it disappeared, delight and distress combined. We may trample on love, curse it, take pleasure in facile pathos, but it is nonetheless love and love alone that gives us the feeling of living at high altitude and, in the moments when it enthralls us, of experiencing in a condensed form all the most precious stages in a destiny. Passion may be doomed to misfortune, but it is a still greater misfortune never to have known passion. ■

PART II

Idyll and Discord

CHAPTER 4

The Noble Challenge of Marriage for Love

To have a proper notion of the abyss of pain in which women have been forced to live, one has to be or have been married.

FLORA TRISTAN, *Les Pérégrinations d'une paria*, 1837

Today, I received two text messages from my girlfriend. The first to tell me that it was all over, the second to tell me that she had sent the message to the wrong address.

On the website Viedemerde.fr, 2008

To find reasons for living, I tried to destroy my reasons for loving you. To find reasons for loving you, I lived badly.

PAUL ÉLUARD, *La Vie immediate*, 1932

In the nineteenth century, an old lady lying on her deathbed in a chateau in Normandy remembers the brilliant years of her youth. At her side, her granddaughter, her blond hair in braids, is reading her the news in the local papers. Nothing but tragic events involving jealousy, a wife who throws vitriol in the face of her husband's mistress, a shopgirl who shoots her faithless young lover. The grandmother, who finds these incidents revolting, laments the disappearance of the Old Regime's gallantry:

> Listen, girl, to an old woman who has seen three generations and who knows a great deal about men and women. Marriage and love have nothing to do with each other. One gets married in order to found a family, and one founds a family in order to constitute society. Society cannot get along without marriage. If society is a chain, each family is a link. To weld those links, similar metals are always being sought.... One gets married only once, my girl, because the world requires it, but one can be in love twenty times in life because nature made us that way. Marriage is a law, you see, and love is an instinct that pushes us sometimes to the right, sometimes to the left. Laws have been made to combat our instincts, and they were necessary, but instincts are always stronger, and one shouldn't resist them too long because they come from God, whereas laws come only from men.

The girl, frightened by these remarks, cries out: "Oh, grandmother, one can love only once . . . marriage is sacred." The old lady then contrasts the civility of the old aristocracy with the current romantic nonsense that has dampened all the joys of life:

> You believe in equality and eternal passion. People have written poems to tell you that you will die of love. In my time, people wrote poetry to teach men how to love all women. And we women. . . , when

our hearts were swept away by some new whim, we wasted no time in dismissing the preceding lover.

The strength of this story by Guy de Maupassant[1] is that it mixes up periods to produce a kaleidoscopic effect. For today's reader, the most retrograde of the two characters is not the one that one might expect, and the unworthy grandmother proves to be more free in her remarks than the girl corseted in an impenetrable idealism. We might be tempted to reconcile the two points of view. Like the adolescent, we believe in marriage for love; like the old lady, we sanctify fervor at the expense of duration, we know that one can fall in love several times in the course of one's life. We waver between two conceptions of conjugal happiness: one consisting of quietude, the other of ardor. The modern couple has become its own principal concern, its sole torment, its most cherished child. That is its beauty, and its tragedy.

Passion Challenged, Passion Praised

Marriage, in the canonical form it has taken in the Western world, was born in a climate of suspicion and revolt; too lubricious for some, too suffocating for others. St. Paul said it all when he reduced the union of the sexes to a lesser evil:

> To the unmarried and the widows I say that it is well for them to remain single as I do. But if they cannot exercise self-control, they should marry. For it is better to marry than to be aflame with passion. (Corinthians 7:8)

For St. Jerome, writing in the fourth century, "nothing is more despicable than loving one's wife as a mistress." Any husband who is too much in love with his spouse and has intercourse with her when she is "impure" or pregnant is an adulterer. One must abstain from the labor of creation during fallow periods.[2] For St. John Chrysostom, marriage's raison d'être is less procreation than the regulation of concupiscence by avoiding suspect physical contacts.

A parallel tradition that stretches from the Provençal troubadours to nineteenth-century feminists and utopians would reject the institution of marriage in the name of equality and passion. In this view, conjugal union combines the vileness of a commercial transaction with the oppression of women. Contracted against the will of the wife, who is bound to a stranger she does not love with the blessing of priests and moralists, it reduces the human being to the status of a commodity and constitutes, according to George Sand, "one of the most barbarian institutions that society has ever begun." Balzac's novels are full of these villainous deals that involve frail girls being sold to repellent old men, arrangements of convenience that are transformed into life sentences.[3] The demand for marriage based on love emerged from the rebellion against this "legal prostitution" (Stendhal) that flouted half the human race. Not until the end of the nineteenth century did public authorities finally understand the urgency of a union founded on mutual attraction and respect.

For a noble of the Old Regime, showing overt affection for his wife would have seemed the height of the ridiculous. If there was love, it had to be declared, as did the husband of the Princess of Cleves, only when one was about to die.[4] Conjugal tenderness might emerge after the wedding as a level-headed emotion that matured over time. Montaigne had summed it up: "A good marriage, if such there be, avoids the company and conditions of love."* Inversely, as we have already seen, the modern family that arose between the seventeenth and the twentieth centuries was based on the growing affection that binds the parents to their children. This model, shaped by a middle class in full expansion, made the home a small sentimental community that isolated itself from the rest of society. The precious women writers of the early seventeenth century were already dreaming of a kind of marriage in which Venus and Cupid triumphed while at the same time freeing women from the burden of repeated pregnancies. This utopia slowly advanced in France and in Europe at large: civil marriage was established on September 20, 1792, along with the right to divorce, depriving the Church of its long-standing control over that institution. The Concordat of 1801 reestablished religious marriage without abolishing civil marriage, but in 1816 the Restoration abolished divorce, which was not authorized again until 1884! With the Third Republic, love became a republican virtue in opposition to the immorality of the Old Regime and marriage became a patriotic act that reconciled spouses, children, and the nation: there might be a *mésalliance* of social conditions but never of the heart![5] Finally, by decreasing the fees and the formalities of the ceremony, a law enacted in France on June 21, 1907, allowed young people to get married without their parents' consent and thus opened the way to the matrimonial

---

*Translator's note: I give here D. M. Frame's translation, *The Complete Essays of Montaigne*, Stanford, CA: Stanford University Press, 1965, p. 647.

paradise.[6] Formerly stigmatized as a fatal illness, passion was now required as the basis for a strong marriage.

Then began the cycle in which we are still living today. For the last three or four centuries, we have seen in Europe a series of historical dissociations: civil marriage was dissociated from religious marriage by ceasing to be a sacrament and becoming a contract. The married couple was dissociated, leading to the legislative authorization of common-law marriage in the 1970s. Finally, marriage itself was made problematic by the invention of all sorts of alternative formulas, including the "Pacte civil de solidarité" or Pacs, a civil pact of domestic partnership) established in France in 1999 that guaranteed the transmission of property from one partner to another, but also accelerated the fluidity of the couple: one can separate from one's partner unilaterally by sending a registered letter to the clerk of the district court. (In its way, the Pacs rehabilitated mutual repudiation.[7]) Multiple kinds of affective bonds are now in competition, accentuating the decline of marriage (but not of maternity, which is flourishing more than ever, at least in France): more than 400,000 marriages were celebrated in 1970, while in 2008 there were only 273,000, for a decrease of 30 percent. Similarly, in 1970 there were twelve divorces per hundred marriages, and in 2006 there were forty-two.[8]

In short, in some Western European countries marriage has become pointless, because its avatars have been multiplied and the couple has ceased to be the canonical form of love. Our desire to take advantage of both states is so strong that the borderline between being married and being unmarried is becoming increasingly vague. It is now possible to have probationary love affairs, on weekends or on vacation, to practice affective make-shifts, taking something from each model without suffering from any. Instead of the conjugal straitjacket, a light coat that one can change at will, chance coalitions. The couple is gradually freeing itself from the three principles that were basic to the classical marriage: publicness, stability, and solemnity. Or rather it wants to have these three things and their contraries, recognition without the consequences that flow from it, eternity in theory and casualness in practice.

We know the old refrain sung by famous authors[9]: passion no longer exists, it was killed by women's liberation, the consumerist hedonism that makes the universe "liquid" (Zygmunt Bauman) and breaks the most sacred bonds. The exactly opposite hypothesis might be advanced: we are living in a hypersentimental period and today couples die because they put themselves under the jurisdiction of a cruel and merciless god—Love. It is not only whims and selfishness that put an end to couples, but also the quest for a permanent passion as the cement that will hold them together. It is the mad intransigence of these lovers or spouses who reject any compromise: either fervor or flight, no half-measures.

The Conformism of Mad Love

For those who tried to conceive it, from Engels to twentieth-century theoreticians (Bertrand Russell, Léon Blum), the love-marriage presented itself as the solution to the two plagues constituted by adultery and prostitution. Combined with social revolution, associating freedom with attraction, it was supposed to change the face of humanity. In France, two names are prominent in this admirable defense of sentiment: Denis de Rougemont and André Breton. On the one hand, the great Swiss historian, hailed by Sartre as early as 1938, is an indefatigable advocate for fidelity and does not allow the word *marriage* to be written in the plural. He quotes with horror a young female millionaire from Texas who told journalists on the eve of her wedding: "It's marvelous getting married for the first time" (she divorced a year later).[10] For him, engaging in matrimony requires something other than a "beautiful fever": a total commitment that presupposes that the future man and wife will retain their composure for life. On the other hand, in 1937 the pope of surrealism, André Breton, defended mad love, "the great nuptial flight . . . that bears the greatest hopes and has been depicted in art for the past twenty centuries," and invited people to "free themselves in love from any concern foreign to love, from any fear, from any doubt." This magnificent plea, which ends with the famous apostrophe addressed to his daughter Aube, who had been born in 1935 ("I hope you will be loved madly"), is accompanied by a stupefying conservatism on the moral level, especially with regard to inconstancy and homosexuality. Breton offers this astonishing analysis of infidelity:

> If the choice was really free, then for the person who made it, it cannot be contested, on any pretext whatever. Guilt starts there and not elsewhere. Here I reject the excuse of habituation, weariness. Mutual love,

as I envisage it, is composed of mirrors that reflect to me, from the countless angles that the unknown can take for me, the faithful image of the woman I love, ever more surprising in divining my own desire and more gilded with life.[11]

Strip away the pompous lyrical trappings and you have the Vatican's doctrine regarding the indissolubility of marriage (though Breton himself married several times).

This is a well-known phenomenon in the history of ideas: secular reformers, on the pretext of challenging the old order, often limit themselves to rigidifying its commandments. They do not overthrow the rule, they reconstruct it as an intransigent utopia.[12] Based on an oath that people impose on themselves, the love-marriage is a union of a superior morality that has to prevail over the vagaries of the heart or the impetuosity of desire. For Rousseau, a great enemy of adultery (whereas he himself had more or less Platonic love affairs with married women[13]), the nuptial bond was already "the most inviolable of all contracts," not to be broken "on any pretext," to the point that we must "shower hatred and curses on anyone who soils its purity." That is because the love commitment generates an absolute requirement. Denis de Rougemont was well aware of this tension. The fidelity that spouses owe each other cannot be subordinated to their happiness but only to a insane truth, a "madness of sobriety" that requires "a patient and tender application," "a life-giving irrigation" in every instant. A strange eulogy for marriage that joins it to the order of unreason: once for all and forever, as Kierkegaard said about religious conversion.

The Couple as Pornographers

Past centuries disassociated the matrimonial bond from pleasure. "Marriage is a religious and holy bond. That is why the pleasure we derive from it should be a restrained pleasure, serious, and mixed with some austerity; it should be a somewhat discreet and conscientious voluptuousness."* If lustful pleasures were to be banned from the conjugal bed, the reason was less a condemnation of instinct than a mistrust of its fragility. Only a well-tempered affection and disciplined emotions could go the distance. Our ancestors were less "prudish than prudent" (Edward Shorter). People might love and desire elsewhere, but the transmission of property and the concern for descent remained the primordial considerations. These are no longer our concerns: aside from the fringes of the most retrograde religious minorities in Europe and the United States, we enjoy complete latitude in choosing, marrying, and leaving whomever we wish. There is no longer any constraining collectivity or father to keep two people from giving themselves to each other. In earlier times, pleasure and the hearth still turned their backs on each other: "A few exceptional happy people note the unhappiness of the multitude caught in the conjugal trap," Charles Fourier said. Now we associate companionship with shamelessness. Intimacy is no longer a place where partners find refuge from the brutality of the world, it is a place of experimentation and fantasy where they elaborate their peculiar pornography.

*Translator's note: I cite Frame's translation, p. 147.

In the nineteenth century, the main obstacle to a conjugal sexuality was the masculine bipolarity analyzed by Freud, which idealized the wife the better to demean the prostitute: with his wife, a man had very brief, domestic relations, especially since the lack of contraception put women at the risk of being fertile at the wrong time,[14] whereas with a prostitute, he had sensual escapades and the whole range of the most unsuitable positions. A mother with a family could not moan like a vulgar streetwalker. The romantic cult of feminine purity led to the explosion of brothels, idealism to whoring. In the second half of the nineteenth century, reformers who wanted to eradicate bad morals recommended that "the bedroom become the exclusive place for love. . . , a victory over the cabaret, the bar, and other disreputable places."[15] Extended to all classes, this movement sought to eliminate the shortage of eroticism in couples and to dry up the venal supply of sex, which was favored by the sexual proletariat of students and bachelors too poor to get married. What religion condemned, reason ultimately established, and a new politics of conjugal pleasure, supervised by medicine, ended up supplanting the old supervision of pleasure.[16] Debauchery and daring acts that were formally experienced with prostitutes were now supposed to take place between man and wife; naughty behavior was to migrate from the brothel to the conjugal bed. Whereas the whorehouse eventually became a place of optimally efficient coitus—one doesn't make love with a prostitute, one empties one's vesicles, and red-light districts are in fact not red-hot but icy-cold. It is now married couples who deviate from conventional behavior and engage in all sorts of passionate follies. Sexual harmony is thus not new; what is new is the excessive hopes that are pinned on it. Love affairs have become a major concern for everyone. The liberation of morals has inverted the priorities in the act of love: it used to be all over once the woman had yielded; now everything begins when she puts her clothes back on. Rejected as macho, men are more than ever in demand as lovers; but they have to have the appropriate equipment and savoir-faire, especially since women are no longer ashamed to flaunt their pleasure. A woman is also expected to have certain competencies that are duly listed. If she is silly or clumsy, there will be no shortage of unpleasant commentaries. Contemporary eroticism is completely subject to a morals of heroic feats. Lovers have to give one another pleasure; otherwise the amorous pair turns into a couple of plaintiffs. Woe to whoever botches the job! In this domain more than in any other, we remain beneficiaries demanding our due.

Sexuality has been assigned a new mission: to measure the married couple's degree of felicity. Since the couple has retained only one of its former roles, namely self-fulfillment, it inquires of eroticism, its new oracle, how it is doing. Sex is not frightening; on the contrary, it is reassuring, it makes love calculable and converts fleeting intensities to memorable sequences. In the enclosed space of their bedroom, lovers prove before their inner tribunal that they are really together. Today, what is a pornographic film if not the last of the household fine arts, alongside cooking and gardening? Couples eager to spice up their sex lives watch porn, or even film themselves having sex, alone or with their neighbors, and put the highlights on the Internet. And since sentiment is not the contrary of desire but its twin in fragility—the trend toward loving tenderness is no less volatile than that toward sensuality—the mission of testing the solidity of conjugal bonds is entrusted to the transports of the flesh.

A whole pedagogy of disinhibition is set up that seeks to unburden us of our reticences. Even at the highest levels of the state,[17] courses are given by specialists to teach us how to stimulate the perineum, how to keep one's pelvic floor fit, how to open up one's "chakras" (centers of energy), how to learn the art of intimate caresses. To learn about another's body, one begins with one's own, masturbation becomes a propaedeutic for coitus, an exercise in self-mastery and self-knowledge. Even help provided by physicians, psychiatrists, and conjugal trainers to encourage sensual frenzy by every means possible is not considered excessive. This involves an extension of the school and the business enterprise to an extracurricular subject, the obligation to produce a result put in the service of wildness. A development that is preferable to the earlier ignorance, but that makes sexuality the crucible for a veritable heroism on the part of the couple. Scientists are working on a mathematical model for pleasure, opening laboratories for marital relations, claiming that they can predict divorces.[18] and producing algorithms of happiness. Curiosity about unknown aspects of the libido is increased by the concern that in any case we are not doing all we could.

We are basing our lives on a myth of eroticism as a kind of tourism. Lovers are travelers who are asked to choose between two kinds of tours: the classical one, with the missionary position and assured comfort, and the adventurous one, which offers the whole range of bizarre practices, spanking on talcum-powdered buttocks, bondage, trios, sodomy, etc. The point is to try out the most unbridled practices, the way one visits faraway places, the Caribbean, China, or Tanzania. With whom can you launch out into depravation other than your beloved spouse who knows you, cuddles with you, and gives you a big kiss after a furious session of S&M? The sensible site of unreasonable actions, the modern couple is the very figure of ambiguity: an image of conformism and of the least commendable fornication. The modern couple practices in high doses what might be called a sentimental obscenity, mixing sweet words with crude ones. The night table becomes an annex to the sex shop, a depository of sexy underwear and various prostheses. (The best fantasies, let us not forget, are always the most primal.) What does it matter that these deviancies are generally fairly minor and remain, despite the ambient permissiveness, relatively confidential? The important thing is that they have entered, via the media, into the collective imagination and form the common horizon of contemporary sexuality.

Chaste in Spite of Ourselves

What terrifies modern spouses is the prospect of seeing their togetherness degenerate into a union of two eunuchs resembling "two railway cars left on the tracks that collide in the amorous act" (Zeruya Shalev). Thus we can understand the role of the sexologist, of the coach, of a former porn star like Brigitte Lahaie, all of whom have been transmogrified into professors of pleasure on the radio or in the newspapers, whose task is to relieve their clients of guilt, to make all the secrets of sensual delight easily accessible. Mixing a master chef's eagerness to share his culinary recipes with the gravity of the expert who takes your hand and guides you through a complex labyrinth. Half teachers, half sorcerers, they combine a pedagogical model and an initiatory model; whence their pontificating tone that allies seriousness and cuteness and applies to intimate subjects the noble language of education. These matrimonial counselors avoid any desire to shock (except on some radio stations for "young people," which remain in the register of classical bawdiness); they do not seek to be subversive but rather prospective, inviting everyone to run through all the keys of the sensorial keyboard.

"Arouse your desire,"[19] we are adjured every month or every trimester by magazines, so great is our fear of a breakdown of the libido. The extravagant attempt made by contemporary lovers is to combine intensity and duration, fire and water, at the risk of losing both of them. Time exercises its power of dissolution on our maddest desires. Even fiery temperaments end up cooling down someday. Desiring less than the other does is intolerable, I am angry with her that she no longer arouses in me the impulse that used to consume me, that our erotic potential is gradually diminishing. It is not the other person that I have to excuse—she is a poor human being like me—but rather the weakness of our constitution. Lasting sexuality is one of the most touching utopias of the modern world; the crumbling of desire constitutes its tragic side even though it is tended like a sacred flame. There is something poignant about two persons who used to be unable of being alone in a room for more than five minutes without throwing themselves on one another and who later cohabit for years, all passion spent, with the exception of brief intervals. The attempt to persevere in the upper spheres of sensual excess will remain one of the most moving episodes in the history of love in the Western world. Chastity is more efficaciously produced by exhausting the appetites than by repression. This proves once again that we are powerless to control the "biology of the passions" (Jean-Didier Vincent).

The Fine Folly of Married Love

The extravagance of our age consists in this unreasonable dream: everything in one. A single being asked to condense the totality of all my aspirations. Who can fulfill such an expectation (especially since there are people with rich inner worlds and others who are content to live parasitically on them)? The vertiginous increase of divorce rates in Europe is not the result, as is often said, of our selfishness, but rather of our idealism: the impossibility of living together combined with the difficulty of remaining alone. Our couples come to an end not from disappointment but from too lofty an idea of themselves. Nothing remains but love, "the dazzling gaze of the god" (André Breton), and that is the whole problem. We overload the ship, we put so many hopes on it that it ends up sinking. We suffer not because our hearts are too dry but because they are too wet; they are inclined to overflow.

We often hear people say that they still believe in old-fashioned love. But what we should believe in is people, who are vulnerable and imperfect, and not in an abstraction, however admirable. To love love in general more than one loves people themselves is to revel in the ideal. At first excluded from marriage, sentiment corroded it from within, and then imperiled itself by excessive ambition: its voraciousness led to its death. Deprived of the obstacles that kept it alive by restraining it, it was forced to find within itself the means of its own renewal. It died not from being hindered but from succeeding too well. Passion, it is said, is irresistible; alas, it resists everything except itself. In classical tragedy, an impossible attachment is opposed to a cool order; contemporary tragedy is love killed by itself, dying from its own victory. It was by exercising its power that it destroyed itself, its apotheosis was its decline. Our romances have never had such short lives, never have they been so quickly recuperated by the conjugal bed, because nothing prevents them from being fulfilled. A poverty that is more insidious than any other, because it arises from satiation, not from lack.

Here is a very widespread malady at the present time: the infernal quest for the right love object, which disappoints and is replaced by another, which is disqualified in turn and then eclipsed by a third, a fourth, and so on—a series of will-o'-the-wisps that glow and flicker out. We get carried away, we cool down, we are never satisfied. Each time we make promises that go beyond our feelings, we feel those false infatuations Stendhal describes, in which "for one evening you believe you will love someone for the rest of your life." The kindred soul is never beautiful and intelligent enough to retain enough: the Prince Charming turns out to be nothing but a born loser and a nasty trick, the sex bomb a frigid neurotic, an ill-tempered shrew, and all the suitors are rejected. That is our hell, the counterpart of our progress: the impossibility of falling in love with men or women who fulfill our aspirations, not because they are mediocre but because our aspirations are insatiable.

Whence the general panic that strikes both sexes from the age of thirty on: they're scared to death that they will end up sitting alone in the evening in front of their television sets, nibbling on a frozen dinner and waiting for the telephone to ring. That is why we find on the Internet or in specialized parties what might be called the secondhand market, the market for second choices, in which people in difficulty—all of whom have been separated and remarried several times and are floating—conceive a passion for a stranger, repudiate it just as quickly, and end up hanging out with questionable individuals.

Twenty years ago, I met in Madras the Indian writer Raja Rao (who died in 2006), a friend of André Malraux: as a young man he had traveled to France, persuaded that in order to know the essence of love he had to marry a European. In an allegorical novel, *The Serpent and the Rope* (1960), he related this experiment and the failure of his marriage. He had returned to India disappointed by the impatience of Europeans, their desire for a happiness that is as constant as it is complete. He drew from this the following conclusion: "[In India,] we put a cold soup on the fire and it warms up little by little. You put a hot soup in a cold dish and it cools down little by little." The occidental couple suffers from the mythologies of the paroxysm, that is, from the ravages of a frantic romanticism; its fault is to take affections too seriously to tolerate the slightest shortcoming. Would you be prepared to die for those that you love? Above all, I am prepared to live with them: the prose of everyday life implies constancy at every moment and makes it futile to speculate regarding gestures that are as extreme as they are aleatory. In the past, sentimental education was connected with disillusionment; one had to find one's way in the meanders of the heart, avoid the errors of the senses, flee youthful illusions and follow a spiritual and moral itinerary. All our literature now teaches us, on the contrary, how to stir up the flame, how to increase ardor. A major reversal with respect to the classical age: the latter feared the unleashing of fatal passions that bring misfortune, while we fear their cooling, their exhaustion. We decree that the passions are poetry, felicity, and minimize the problems. It is no longer the anarchy of behavior that we fear, it is the disappearance of emotion.

The Old Lovers' Suicide

Toward the end of his life, Chateaubriand fell in love with a young woman who spurned him; in his old age, Casanova was forced (in a novel by Arthur Schnitzler) to disguise himself as a lovebird to seduce a young woman; in Marienbad, at the age of seventy-two, Goethe proposed to a girl of seventeen who refused him; Mrs. Stone (in a book by Tennessee Williams), an American in her eighties, falls in love in Rome with the handsome Paolo, who is scarcely twenty years old, and thinks she is "leading an almost posthumous existence," whereas her life resembles "the cloth of a tent that would collapse in loose folds without the central post that supported it."[20] So many examples that raise the same question: how can we make up our minds to leave the stage? The answer is simple: it is others who give us the

hook, declare that our appetites are unsuitable, that libidi-
nous old men can no longer be allowed to confiscate young
people. (In this domain, nature and prejudices are crueler
for women.)

More moving than these tales about the vanity of old
men and coquettes is the death of old lovers. Some people
are so imbued with one another, so interwoven like the
roots of a tree, that they form a single person endowed
with two faces and two names, a *we* that can no longer be
separated into two *I*'s. Then one's pain becomes the other's
pain. "It is I who suffer when my wife's legs hurt her," the
Spanish philosopher Unamuno said magnificently. It also
sometimes happens that a serious illness that strikes one of
the partners causes the other not to want to go on, and they
resolve to depart together. This happened in September
2007 in the case of André Gorz and his wife, who was afflicted with a degenerative disease: "you have just turned
eighty-two," he had written in a book that was dedicated
to her, "you have lost 6 cm. in height, and you weigh only
45 kg., and yet you are still beautiful, charming, desirable.
We have been living together for fifty-eight years and I love
you more than ever. Recently I fell in love with you again
and once again I am bearing within me an overflowing life
that is fulfilled only when I hold your body in my arms."[21]
Before them, other couples, such as the former socialist
senator Roger Quillot and his wife in 1998, had decided
to depart at the same time, preparing their farewells like
conspirators, and finding gaiety and serenity before bringing down the curtain. (Unfortunately, the pills they took
did not kill Claire Quillot, and she had to know the terrible
experience of solitude.) Why let nature separate you from
the only person who counts when one can make the last
journey together? Better to make the end come earlier than
undergo decline. Suicide, John Donne said, absolves itself,
since unlike sin it can be committed only once.

There is something worse than our own deaths, and that is the death of those close to us, the few fundamental persons who are essential to us. There is no point in surviving them, it is better to leave in time. What is more beautiful in that regard than the myth of Philemon and Baucis, who begged Jupiter to make them die together, and who were transformed into a tree at the end of their lives? There is perhaps more grandeur in the suicide of old lovers than in the noisy love-making of the young. Youth is demonstrative, but old age is sublime. "I shall be dust, but amorous dust"[22] (Quevedo).   ■

CHAPTER 5

Fluctuating Loyalties

I should blush for the faults that I have committed;
I long for those I can no longer commit.

PIERRE ABELARD

We find it innocent to desire and atrocious that the
other desires.

MARCEL PROUST

Beware of a brother, for every brother can be a Jacob,
every friend spreads calumny, one dupes the other.
Fraud upon fraud. Deception on deception.

JEREMIAH

In a commune in California, sometime in the 1960s, about
forty boys and girls gathered in accord with the principles
of the strictest sexual communism: forming an established
couple was prohibited, partners were to be rotated, and
preference based on aesthetic or cultural criteria was rejected. At the end of a year, some of the members who were
obese or ugly found that they were being refused access to
other members' bedrooms and started wandering about on

the veranda during the evening, begging for a bed and repeating: who wants me?

There is no stronger argument for traditional marriage
than this absolute counterexample. Conservatives will say
that it shows the victory of good sense over the divagations
of the 1960s. And they will cite Jean Paulhan's famous bon
mot: "I had a friend who did not want to marry: when one
marries, one has to give up all women but one. I knew exactly how to answer him: when one does not marry, one
gives up all women plus one."[1] The sophism is cute, but
doesn't hold up: one can marry and love several times in
a life, experience a successive polygamy or polyandry, and
the choice is never between one person or no one. Above
all, in the more developed parts of the Western world, one
can lead a full affective life without marrying. At each end
of the world of love's spectrum, we find fierce partisans:
strong supporters of monogamy or of promiscuity urge us
to follow their example on pain of malediction.

The battle between these two parties is somewhat tiresome. The couple is no more an end to be pursued than is
free love; it is simply the contingent form that our attachments take at a given moment in our lives. What is truly
new about our time is that we no longer have to choose
between untenable injunctions; in the course of a lifetime
we can experience marriage, celibacy, and brief flings. That
is why the question of fidelity is both fundamental and in-
soluble: it is so difficult to be constant, and so tricky not
to be. The liberation of morals obliges us to construct our
own rules. When society delegates to individuals the problems that formerly fell within its purview, it assigns them
a task they don't know how to cope with. To free oneself is

always to burden oneself. Just imagine how complicated it is to subject the most intense love to the test of a major illness or an economic setback: how many men thrown out of work are abandoned by their companions, how many persons suffering from long-term maladies become a burden for those around them, who end up hoping that death will come soon? We are neither heroes nor saints, just ordinary humans with limited capacities for devotion.

Boorishness, the Offspring of Sincerity

The crisis in middle-class marriage is supposed to have led to a depreciation of one of its most common derivatives: adultery. Formerly condemned in the name of good morals, it is now condemned in the name of sincerity. The free association of two individuals cannot accommodate such a petty practice: it is better to tell each other everything than to resort to the subterfuges of an earlier time. Making people laugh at the misfortunes of cuckolded husbands was a mainspring of boulevard theater for almost a century, and the cuckold has always been a character in vaudeville.[2] However, adultery, even if it is discredited, is not dead: outdated as a genre, it remains current as a practice and is one of the main reasons for the breakdown of marriages.[3] Adultery is practiced by both men and women who deceive one another to combat boredom, to respond to temptations, or to lead several lives at once; it is a symptom of an individualist society torn between the ideal of fidelity and a thirst for freedom. It continues to be indissolubly connected with the couple. Here again two discourses

are determined to demolish it: one normative, one inno-
vative. The former, the discourse of psychoanalysis, sees
it as a symptom of an unresolved childhood tension. For
example, Aldo Naouri tells us that adultery can be written
in basic Lacanian: "adulte erre, adulte taire," an errant and
lost adult who holds his tongue in order not to grow up. We
think we are flirting freely, but we are prey to an excessive
attachment to the mother or the father.[4] Another school of
psychoanalysis deplores, in the old word *deception*, a self-
denial, an atmosphere of mendacity that corrupts our most
cherished affections. Having begun with extravagant promises, the couple bogs down in wretched hypocrisies.

The first objection calls upon us to respect the moral law,
the second to respect the private, intimate law. There are
now two fidelities: one a fidelity of convention, the other
a fidelity of conviction. The former involves a mechanical
observance of social norms, the second a free decision to be
loyal to one's beloved. The latter can be subdivided into the
fidelity we owe to the other and that we owe to ourselves.
The ardent obligation to remain in accord with one's own
whims makes the question more complex. There is a new
malice in our love affairs: my attachment to myself autho-
rizes me to stab the other in the back. In the name of the
absolute right to change my mind, I can break my word.
The omnipotence of the turnaround: if I've slept with X or
Y, that is because at that time I no longer loved you, I'd had
enough of pretending to have feelings for you. (What do
our rivals in love, whether men or women, have that we
don't have? One thing for sure: they are new. That is what
makes them irresistible, not their beauty or their minds.)
The person betrayed can no longer invoke a repressive

society: the partner's misbehavior is an affront, and "cuckoldry" becomes a personal failure: if our mates want to seek
their amorous sustenance elsewhere, that is because we are
no longer enough for them.

To be responsible only for oneself is thus to be disagreeable in the highest degree. I no longer retract, I evolve, a
higher virtue commands me to renounce my commitments, I am unfaithful out of fidelity to myself. The treachery of the renegade who tramples on his engagements becomes, by way of a sophism, the highest form of ethics. If
all it takes to be right is to be oneself, the modern cult of
authenticity leads straight to the triumph of insensitivity.
To be in harmony with ourselves, it commands us to reject
all hypocrisy, all obligation to show concern for the other.[5]
As soon as an interlocutor warns you that he is going to
be sincere, you can expect an avalanche of disagreeable remarks. Insensitivity is the opposite of gallantry: it consists
in treating the other as an instrument to be cast aside once
it has been used.

The Proper Use of Reticence

The mysticism of transparency resembles persecution:
keeping the other up to date on my doubts, the slightest
tremors of my heart, like a seismologist, is like constantly
riddling her with bullets. The politics of confession is first
of all a politics of malice: to speak of everything is to speak
ill, whereas reticence is connected with the principle of
delicacy. I am grateful to the other for concealing some of
his thoughts from me. How often would we prefer not to

know, and say, as Monsieur de Cleves does to his wife on his deathbed: "Why did you not leave me in the calm blindness in which so many husbands are happy?"[6] We know Kant's apologue about a man pursued by killers who takes refuge in a house. The owner of the house has a duty, Kant says, to betray him in the name of the universality of the moral law: lying is always and everywhere wrong.[7] Benjamin Constant, commenting ironically on this example, opposed to it the no less irrepressible duty to save another person's life. To tell one's spouse the truth and nothing but the truth, as one would do in a court of law, is to subject her to an unbearable pressure. Here there is an inversion of classical morality: while one lies, one does so because one cares for the other and safeguarding the relationship is more important than the need to confess. To keep quiet is to protect; to confess is to devastate. Against cruel frankness, we must defend the principle of kindness and discretion. In a couple, there is a good way to make use of duplicity: vagueness in confiding is better than the probity of the confessional.

Not to mention that deception has an incontestable erotic potential: the fear of being caught, spur-of-the-moment rendezvous, and shared secrets lend some clandestine encounters a density that the conjugal gruel no longer has. We sometimes lie not to conceal the truth but to make life more intense. Consider in Proust the extravagant fables created by the beloved woman to protect herself against her lover's attentions, as the cuttlefish exudes ink in order to drive unwanted creatures away. In this case, her wildest stories prove to be true. There is a kind of giddiness of betrayal with respect to relatives, spouses, friends: we stab in the back only those who are close to us and whose weak points we know. The intimate sphere is also the site of the worst treacheries. There is something fascinating about the villainy of the shady schemes cooked up by lovers conspiring to destroy one another. So far as we know, the passion for robbery felt by a thief waiting in ambush has miraculously not disappeared from the couple. There are conjugal parasites who are constantly trying to throw a wrench into the strongest marriages. (Life in common is often tolerable only in the framework of a mysterious free rider who represents the vanishing point. The lovers' triangle then becomes the condition for the couple's happiness.) Looking around among one's spouse's best friends in order to deceive her (or him) transforms proximity into promiscuity, and redoubles the giddy pleasure taken in cheating by adding the piquancy of familiarity. It is the whole paradox of malevolent contiguity that constructs a strong bond the better to destroy it. Confidence leads to betrayal, and the traitor has always begun by being a brother, a companion.

There are many ways of being disloyal without committing an offense with a third party: by withdrawing into oneself, by withholding sex, a smile, or conversation. Strict respect for physical fidelity can be somewhat neurotic in its rigidity: the energy expended on avoiding faux pas is exerted to the detriment of the love given the person for whom one seeks to make such efforts. It seems that Mahatma Gandhi liked to spend the night alongside naked women to test his resistance. Some people think they are faithful who are merely lazy and prefer their quiet Sundays to the hassles involved in brief encounters. Others enjoy temptation in order to resist it, and like to teeter on the edge of the abyss: they flirt with strangers and then draw back. They do not love their husbands or wives; they love their power of seduction and their strength of character. With the Psalmist, they could say: "Prove me, O Lord, and try me; test my heart and my mind" (Psalms 26:2). This is also the problem of the tease who drives men mad without ever giving them anything. Denis de Rougemont tells with admiration this anecdote about one of his women friends. She had flirted in vain with a married man, and as he left her he said: "I am adding you to my list of the *mille e tre*." These were the women he hadn't had out of fidelity to his wife.[8] That is an exercise characteristic not of a stable heart, but of a boastful one that wants get drunk on its strength without using it. It is vanity disguising itself as a moral law. "The violence one does oneself to remain faithful to what one loves is hardly better than an infidelity," La Rochefoucauld said.

Prohibit Prostitution?

Socialists and feminists expected the disappearance of the middle-class family to put an end to the problem of prostitution. The latter was seen as a plague that education and social revolution would eliminate. In 1936, Wilhelm Reich predicted that the entry of young women into sexual life would signal the end of pornography and sexual slavery. It is true that today women are incontestably freer, at least in democratic countries, and yet prostitution continues to be rampant. We can find countless reasons, both good and bad, for this persistence, but there is one that is dominant: there will always be a group of people involved in mercenary sex because freedom does not guarantee the fair distribution of sensual pleasure and too many individuals do not have access to it because of their poverty, their appearance, or their age.

It is pointless to embellish the fact: prostitution remains an unpleasant and even sordid trade that exposes those who practice it to bullying by their customers, the arbitrary actions of the police, the violence of pimps, and the disapproval of respectable people. Those who engage in it are driven, like any worker, by deprivation and a lack of security, and they prefer this trade to so many others that are equally degrading. Alas, the debate about the subject has come to resemble a genuine witch-hunt conducted by religious fundamentalists, reactionary feminists, and conservatives of the right and left, all of whom have formed a coalition to thrust women who provide entertainment still further into their misery.[9] Formerly disqualified as involved in vice, prostitutes are now seen as victims who have strayed onto the paths of voluntary servitude and for whom treatment has to be provided. They used to be criminalized, now they are infantilized. Associations of "sex workers" can demand better conditions all they want; they are ignored on the ground that they are supposed to be manipulated, simple mouthpieces with no autonomy.

The fact that women, hustlers, and transvestites are fighting not to abolish their trade but to improve it is what dismays the morally self-satisfied. The latter wanted to save them, while their concern is only to normalize their trade. There are in fact two lefts, a liberal left that acknowledges the great diversity of personal choices and seeks to respect them against the background of social advancement, and a punitive, criminalizing left that wants to correct individuals and has only one slogan: punish, correct, straighten out. This latter left, which claims to act in the name of dignity, resembles the Christian cohorts of the Middle Ages who were prepared to kill the infidel, to burn a witch to save her soul.

What should we do, then, if we know that there is no good solution and that in this area we are caught between Scylla and Charybdis? We must choose the lesser evil: manage this trade while respecting the persons who practice it, allow them to enjoy the fruits of their work and especially to leave it when they want to without remaining stigmatized. Protect them against pimps; look on them with favor because they are doing public health work and offering a little happiness to lonely people. A point of convergence for all anxieties, a scandalous supplement, venal sex terrifies a society that thought it had emancipated Eros and now sees that it has not solved problems, but merely complicated them. Thus the only thing we should do is accord the social workers for the libido the same prerogatives that are enjoyed by other employees by freeing them from the malediction in which they are confined by every camp.

We can go further: now that the second sex has become a full-fledged economic actor and holds a certain financial power, why not open houses of male prostitution for women, and authorize women to have sensual interludes for pay with lovers of their choosing? Sexual tourism for women already exists in Africa and in the Caribbean, and there are numerous networks of "call boys." As for the traditional objections—women are too sentimental, they would never engage in anonymous eroticism—they essentialize the feminine and confound cultural conditioning with a fact of nature: women have a libido no less impulsive than men's, and men are no less sentimental than they are. We can bet that if places of pleasure reserved for women open up some day, the customers will still be the ones who are called whores, and will be blamed for seeking a little comfort in exchange for payment. So women are forbidden to be either buyers or sellers of sexual services, a curious anachronism in a time in which a majority of women earn their own livings and want the associated pleasures. Why

are call girls condemned more than gigolos, when they
practice virtually the same trade? We continue to make the
genitals a synecdoche of the female body; we take the part
for the whole. Man has a sexual organ; woman is her sexual
organ. To present her sexual organ as woman herself is to
go astray. A century after Freud, many people still cling to
this archaic prejudice. That explains everything.   ■

Europe, the United States, Different Taboos

We recall the stories that have run in American newspapers
in recent years: the conservative judge Clarence Thomas,
accused in 1991 of having made indecent remarks to one
of his advisors at the Department of Education; the unfortunate Clinton-Lewinsky affair; the tribulations in 2007 of
the governor of New York, Eliot Spitzer, a champion of the
fight against prostitution who was caught with a ravishing
twenty-two-year-old brunette whom he was paying for her
services; the public confession made by his successor for
fear that later on the press would reveal his own infidelities;
and the attacks made in 2008 against the head of the IMF,
Dominique Strauss-Kahn, who had had intimate relations
with one of his former employees.[10] Each time, America
took an intense interest, both on the left and on the right,
in these sexual escapades as though the foundational pact
on which the nation was based had been put in danger. We
no longer ask politicians whether they love their wives but
rather whether they have cheated on them. The transgression comes before the norm. Apart from the amusing spectacle of advocates of decency ending up in the arms of call
girls, the bitterness of the debates is somewhat stupefying

for a Frenchman. People test their partner's strength using "honey traps," sending him or her a tempter assigned to make him or her slip; in the animal realm, the Emperor penguin of the South Pole, a model of sobriety and monogamy, is celebrated; seminars are held for offending couples who are reeducated in the manner of dissidents in the Soviet empire; and family therapy groups are told that the "reactions of a wife who has been betrayed resemble the symptoms of post-traumatic stress experienced by victims of major catastrophes like September 11." Such an analogy strikes French people as grotesque. We can understand that political officials are called upon to be exemplary in their private behavior: a public man does not belong to himself; if he wants to exercise authority over others, he must be able to control his own instincts.[11] But why must this requirement be extended to the ordinary citizen, of whom irreproachable conduct is demanded?

This is a strange reversal, to be sure: it is as if Americans had erased the fundamental theses of British liberalism, those of Mandeville and Adam Smith, who see in the satisfaction of individual vices the driving energy of the public good,[12] whereas during the French Revolution Robespierre tried in vain to establish the "government of virtue." Now we see Americans, forgetting that the separation between the political and the domestic orders is a modern conquest, are trying to construct on the level of morals a society of the Good that would extirpate corruption from the human heart. To prove disloyal in love is almost to put in question the social contract inaugurated in 1787 between people of all conditions, races, and religions, marriage becoming the symbol of the founding oath of the nation. It is as if

Americans' personal self was only a mirror of society: if the little homeland that is the family wobbles as a result of the infringements committed by spouses, what will happen to the great homeland in the event of danger? The conservatives' main argument is that to deceive one's spouse is simply to betray one's country. That is why the confession of the offense is public and takes on the air of a collective expiation in which the people as a whole, through the escapades of its officials, exorcises its fragility, and refounds the norm by castigating its offenses against it.

Why is there this difference between the United States and Europe, and especially France, where the private behavior of heads of state and individuals are far from irreproachable? No doubt a difference in culture: Americans believe in the sacred character of the marriage contract, whereas the French contractualize this sacrament. Americans interpret in accord with the letter of the law; Europeans interpret in accord with the spirit of the law. But above all, the taboos are not the same: in France, because of the Catholic tradition, it is money that is obscene, whereas in America, with its Protestant heritage, it is sex. "Greed is good," one side says; "France is flexible: one can rise even from a couch," says the other (Alphonse de Lamartine). The Anglo-Americans have counterbalanced their religious puritanism with an insatiable thirst for profit. On the one side there is great admiration for financial success, on the other a great tolerance for human weaknesses. And since every moralist someday falls into the vice that she denounces, the French hatred for money does not prevent its elites from being corrupted any more than the Americans' virtuous sermons prevent adultery from flourishing in their country as it does everywhere. It is hard for contemporary societies to accept their share of immorality except in disciplinary, religious, or psychiatric terms. On the moral level, however, one can only urge Americans to learn from the Old World how to be temperate. I am less sure, in these times of crisis, that the French should be inspired by the attraction of profit characteristic of Americans. All in all, fickleness is less dangerous than the cupidity that has brought the world to its knees: Casanova is more likable than Madoff. A strong democracy tolerates the fluidity of connections and individual failures. Asking faultless perseverance of a man or woman is asking him or her to be superhuman: "Below the belt, there is neither fidelity nor law," as a magnificent Italian proverb has it. True fidelity, after all, demands more than strict physical abstinence, and if love is strong, it will overcome these episodes. In his book *Marriage and Morals* (1929), Bertrand Russell advocated a solution in the French manner: great tolerance for brief flings, for both men and women, provided that they in no way interfere in the life of the couple and do not hinder the upbringing of children. Conjugal calm can tolerate the little arrangements between spouses that are the mark of real refinement. Everyone, at least once in his life, has deceived or been deceived, and we can survive our spouses' infidelities, no matter how much they hurt us.

In certain respects, adultery can be seen as the ally and not the adversary of married life: a truce, a way of refounding the bond by means of a few infringements of it. In the eighteenth century, historians tell us, "valentinage," from which Valentine's Day was derived, allowed wives in northern France to make love, on a few days each year and with the knowledge of their husbands, with a "valentine" of their choosing. "Mutually agreed-upon sharing" (Fourier) constitutes a beneficial interlude between spouses: for the brief period of a fleeting love affair, it eases the burden borne by partners without dissolving it, and often strengthens a faltering bond. For example, what is "swinging" if not a technique for resisting the erosion of a marriage by accepting a supervised fling undertaken by one or both of the spouses? We lend another person our wives or husbands for an evening, and keep an eye on them the better to take them back afterward. Controlled cheating is better than uncontrollable love-making. I knew a couple who went to swingers' clubs only on one condition: they would not kiss casual partners on the lips. All fantasies were allowed except touching lips. If one of them forgot the rule, a quarrel resulted and the couple, naked as Adam and Eve, heaped abuse on each other amid embracing bodies. Where will possessiveness find its niche?

The Mad Delight of Investigation

It is generally accepted that jealousy is a very base sentiment that combines emotional insecurity with a thirst to appropriate; it often ends in a kind of cannibalism and prefers to devour the partner symbolically rather than to see him escape. Even if it could imprison the beloved in a dungeon, it would still worry about his dreams, his sleep. For some people, it becomes a way of life that combines suspicion and investigation, which alone are capable of restarting the motor of love. The compulsively jealous person creates the crime before it is committed and often the actual offense relieves his pain rather than reviving it. It seems that he almost wishes for this treachery that he claims to abhor. We take pleasure in the fact that every jealous person ends up provoking what he fears.

It remains that once this sentiment has been analyzed in all its pettiness, it still cannot be eradicated by the stroke of a pen. Claiming to cleanse the passions of their nasty aspects amounts to assimilating the couple to a parliament in which each person's desires are put through the sieve of deliberation or voting. For example, the right to look elsewhere is demanded, and the other is asked to recognize in good faith that one has that right, on the condition that it is reciprocal. We might have doubts about this portrait of open marriage repainted in the hues of paradisiacal socialism. In order for suffering to disappear, we would have to suppose a simultaneity of appetites and satisfactions in each of the two partners, a homogeneous temporality that offers them identical opportunities to satisfy their craving with a stranger. What if one of them spends the night with a somebody picked up in a bar, while the other spends it alone, at home? We get the odd impression that reformers seek less to ensure lovers' pleasure than to correct the ambiguities of sentiment. They distrust versatility, want to correct people: say everything and hide nothing.[13] But it is another romantic illusion of fusion that is at play here, the illusion of the communion of souls that make themselves clear to one another: interminable discussions, the rejection of secrecy, adjustments. The same principle governs the politics of "open space" in the world of work: offices without walls in which everyone works in full view of everyone else, the main effect being that no one any longer communicates.

But jealousy is also a fellow traveler of democratic equality: it is closely related to the desire for ubiquity, the will to be simultaneously everywhere one is not, and it is not only the fear of being deceived, but also a kind of vertigo that occurs when we are confronted by the opacity of the other, who will remained closed to us no matter what happens. I will never settle down in her brain as I might in the cockpit of an airplane and control her as I wish, see the world through her eyes, know her destiny. There are countless other possible lives that I will never know and that expropriate me of my own.

We are not about to abandon the absurd desire of possession. We are divided between two kinds of jealousy: jealous of our independence and jealous of the other, we construct ephemeral compromises between these two postulates, living in a kind of minor exclusivity that is both imperious and very accommodating. A double life, a ménage à trois, swinging groups, separate vacations, recourse to call girls or toy boys—the contemporary couple shows sufficient flexibility to admit into the duo beneficial third parties who may put it in peril but who may also renew it. Paid sexual services available to both partners authorize sexual diversity without the complications of adultery. Money is a disinfectant that strips these sensual interludes of any affective ambiguity. As in former days, the subterranean life of the conjugal duo (pornography, prostitution, swinging, adultery) supports its legal life, sublime love draws its strength from the reserves of clandestinity, from the illicit. And this remains secret, sheltered from statistics. (It is often objected that young people are returning massively to monogamy and constancy. There is no evidence for this pious hope: young people, despite their desire to break with the cheap dreams of the 1960s, have romances that are no less stormy than those of their elders. To imagine that upcoming generations are going to change life radically amounts to begging the question: they begin by reproducing inherited behaviors and even their dissent reminds us of that of their parents.)

People have scoffed at the Sartre–Simone de Beauvoir pair, criticized their inaugural pact, their distinction between contingent and necessary loves (directly inspired by Fourier), their ambition to be involved with several others without ceasing to be with one another; people have reproached them for having smuggled into their group boys and girls that they exchanged, as in dispersed harems, and who became the dupes of their manipulations. Simone de Beauvoir herself admitted it: "There is one question that we thoughtlessly avoided: how would a third party deal with our arrangement? It happened that he adapted to it without difficulty: our union left enough room for friendships or amorous companionships, for fleeting romances. But if the protagonists demanded more, conflicts broke out. On this point, a necessary discretion compensated for the intense excitement of the scenes depicted in *La Force de l'âge*."[14] It has been maliciously pointed out that despite their audacity, they were conventional lovers, suffered the agonies of bitterness and disappointment. What torments, what splitups they endured in order finally to grow old together and remain loyal, not to their original pact, but to one another![15] I know of few couples as exemplary in that they embody the contradictions with which we all struggle.

The end of passionate avant-gardes. All the proposed remedies for the ills of marriage limited themselves to surreptitiously reproducing them. It is as hard to be completely constant as to be completely inconstant: one would have to remain faithful to this infidelity, which would be logically self-contradictory. If certain spouses strike, with certain conditions, the clause of sexual exclusivity, it would be absurd to make this an imperative: it is for each person to work out his arrangements, knowing full well that something that involves arbitrating between the need for security and the need for adventure can never be raised to the level of a solution. In any case, this oscillation between betrayals and loyalty does not present itself as a model. In the end, the worst infidelity a couple can commit is with regard to itself: by showing itself unworthy of the rush of feeling that bore it and allowing drab, tedious repetitiveness to overcome the mad intoxication of its beginnings.

The Domestic Quarrel, a Category of Purgation

There are several kinds of malice in our love lives, but one of them is particularly cruel: explaining how fate has loosened a bond. That's the way it is, there's nothing we can do about it. Valmont, announcing his departure to Mme de Tourvel, provides a dazzling demonstration:

> We get bored with everything, my angel, it's a law of nature: it's not my fault. So now if I'm bored by an affair which has completely absorbed me for four solid months, it's not my fault. If, for instance, the extent of my love has exactly matched the extent of your virtue—and that's certainly saying a great deal—it's

not surprising that they have both run out at the same time. It's not my fault. The result is that I've been deceiving you for some time now; but in fact it was your dogged devotion which somehow forced me to! It's not my fault. Now a woman whom I desperately love is insisting that I give you up. It's not my fault. I'm well aware that this gives you an excellent opportunity to cry foul; but if nature granted men only constancy while endowing women with stubbornness, it's not my fault. Take my advice, do like me and get yourself another lover. This is good advice, in fact, it's very good advice: if you don't like it, it's not my fault. Farewell, my angel. I've enjoyed having you and I have no regrets at leaving you. I may come back to you. That's the way of the world. It's not my fault.[16]

In opposition to this fatalism, the domestic quarrel remains the most common therapy for purging the couple of its bad blood. There are couples that survive only by means of daily eruptions of fury, and that alternate between bearing the burdens of everyday life and having convulsions of anger. They enjoy the comfort of eternal squabbling. They need these attacks of hysteria to reweld their bonds, the way others need their pills. Beginning or ending the day with a good fight is the best way to avoid falling into a routine. The slow disintegration of love requires the establishment of a stormy area within the quiet harbor. The couple protects us from everything, including love, but to protect itself from itself, it has to put itself in danger. A quarrel wards off real death. The sadness of these old couples who no longer have enough energy to fight with each other, in which what is left unsaid accumulates like dirty dishes in the sink. An amorous peace is a polemical peace, a creative confrontation that transforms friction into union.

The bad faith of complaints in a quarrel is patent, any means is good for reawakening a relationship that is going to seed: tiny details, a vase that has been broken, a paper that has been lost, one contemptuous sniff too many are raised to the level of crimes against humanity. The breaches opened by exasperation are widened, countless reasons for depreciating the other are discovered. A fortunate effect of the quarrel: it allows you to get everything off your chest at once; it has a cathartic power if it remains only a parenthesis. The cartloads of insults that you heap on your spouse, your wounding remarks, would normally separate you from her. But on the contrary they are what will allow you to put up with her in long-term, passionate intimacy. When the quarrel degenerates into a reflex, it throws the lovers into the Hell of permanent aversion. Whatever the other does, it is always bad. Then a binary system is set up: ordinary hatred, insults, roaring, spitting; extraordinary hatred, a symphony of invectives, blows, humiliations, an infernal opera. Such fits of rage soil those whom they touch and especially outside witnesses. The spouses resemble those exhausted troops who have to recoup their strength between two battles before going back to the front. Then they combine two defects, and we know which one is worse: baseness and tedious repetition. They are as repugnant as they are tiresome; they are ratiocinating horror incarnate. ■

CHAPTER 6

The Pleasures and Servitudes
of Living Together

It is not what is criminal that is hardest to say,
it is what is ridiculous and shameful.

JEAN-JACQUES ROUSSEAU, *The Confessions*

So they were both there, happy, useless. . . , depending on each other like supply and demand. . . . Now
what should be done with their victory? Except for
the time when they were washing themselves (and
the special rambling of dreams), they no longer experienced solitude. Between them, there was nothing
fortuitous, touchy, enchanted. They belonged to each
other in the harshest light: that of happiness.

PAUL MORAND, *Lewis et Irène*

I don't always think about those I love, but I claim
that I love them even when I am not thinking about
them, and I would be capable of compromising my
peace of mind in the name of an abstract feeling, in
the absence of any real, instantaneous emotion.

JEAN-PAUL SARTRE, *Situations I*

For the past few years, a strange ceremony has been performed in Paris, on Montmartre's Place des Abbesses. During this ceremony, which takes place during the grape harvest, young couples come to register with an official their "non-demande-en-mariage," that is, their refusal to marry, and to say, as in the Georges Brassens song, "I have the honor of not asking your hand in marriage." There is no ceremony beautiful enough for us, these new-model fiancés seem to be saying, but it is still an official whom they ask to sanction their refusal of an official commitment. They want the symbol without the constraint: a strange way of playing with the institution that is brought in the better to reject it. We have moved beyond marriage as a rule, but we have perhaps not yet left it behind as part of our *imaginaire*.

On a Return to Marriage Lite

We have greatly misjudged the nostalgia for traditional marriage in a white wedding gown. It is a formal nostalgia that smuggles in the thrill of the sacred under the alibi of tradition. We play with signs, we invoke symbols, the horse-drawn carriage, the limousine, a reception in a castle, but as a stage setting. Marriage used to be a condition, analogous to social orders, the clergy, the knighthood: a ritual of initiation, it marked a turning point in one's life. It is becoming renewable and revocable, but for many people it remains an obligatory step. One has to be married at least once, even if the marriage takes place as a consecration after ten years of living together. Even Christian fiancés apply a consumerist logic to the wedding ceremony, because they want it to be performed by a fashionable curate, in a ravishing Romanesque chapel, to the great dismay of the rejected priests.

In 1644, the poet John Milton published a long plea in favor of divorce that was to become the founding document of marriage, not its negation. Milton drew a parallel between the conjugal bond and the relation between the people and the king: just as the charter of a nation may be broken if the sovereign abuses his power, it must be possible to dissolve a marital union in the event of grave discord. If we take marriage seriously, Nietzsche said, we should forbid couples to bind themselves to each other forever, a view that seems even more relevant in a period in which people live to be eighty or even ninety. The good thing about divorce is that it civilizes marriage, which ceases to be a prison: that is why, in Europe at least, 70 percent of the filers for divorce are women, intoxicated by this new possibility. How about partnership? Yes, but with an escape hatch, permission to leave, vanishing points that prevent spouses from feeling suffocated. (Consider the case of an American woman who in 2008 rejected her divorce because the house she owned with her husband had lost half its value. The economic crisis as an auxiliary of the moral order!) To condemn the decay of our morals, people cite as paragons married couples who have been living together for fifteen, twenty, or thirty years; but love is not endurance test, it is certain quality of the bonds between two persons. If this quality persists over time, so much the better, but people do not get married in order to hold out as long as possible and at any cost.

When two people want to live together, they no longer ask their parents' permission or seek their approval. Or if they do ask and are refused, they live together anyway. Thus we will not return to forced marriages, and the depressing spectacle witnessed in some Muslim or traditionalist countries is enough to dissuade us from doing so.[1] The fact that we can choose between traditional marriage, cohabitation, and a free relationship, that in the course of our lives we can encounter several forms of interpersonal connection, is ultimately a major step forward. We have not destroyed the institution of matrimony, we have, like hermit crabs, adapted it to our needs, bent it to our will to the point of making it unrecognizable. The old fortress has not collapsed and remains desirable for many people. Its genius is to have incorporated everything that opposed it—passion, inconstancy, freedom of action. It has drawn strength from what attacked it; it has endlessly diversified itself, so that it is absurd to condemn the couple and to condemn us to live only as a couple. If the conjugal model persists, that is because many individuals find it suitable for them; it has become a potluck, a potpourri of ambitions and expectations that can be open to anyone, including gays and lesbians. But this infiltration has absolute limits. If children are involved, personal choice is no longer the dominant factor. Giving birth to a child is irrevocable and commits the progenitors permanently, beyond the vagaries of the heart. In this domain, the legislator's task is to guarantee the stability of descent, to protect the weakest in order to compensate for conjugal instability: to act in accord with the mores, to be sure, but not at the expense of responsibility. That is the acrobatic feat we have to perform.

On a Conventional Lament

There is a poignant Beatles song, "She's Leaving Home," the story of a girl who runs away in the early morning, leaving a note on the kitchen table. We share the feelings of an adolescent tired of parental mediocrity, and those of the father and mother devastated by this abandonment.

The family used to weigh on us like a leaden mantle; it is now more like a tent full of holes that lets through the wind and rain. That is the most common view of the debacle brought about by the individualist revolution. Isn't it odd that in France this phenomenon coexists with an exceptional fecundity promoted by a judicious governmental policy (day-care centers, parental leaves) that makes work for women no longer the enemy but the ally of high birth rates? France has succeeded, better than Germany, in achieving the delicate combination of professional success and maternity, even if women are now giving birth in their mid-thirties.[2] Isn't it astonishing that the deterioration of matrimonial ties goes hand in hand with an increasing desire to "found a family," even on the part of those who were traditionally deprived of that possibility, namely members of minorities? On this level, the conservatives' lament is out of touch with reality: our democracies are reconstituting on different bases what they earlier destroyed. They are showing a remarkable homeostasis between experimentation and prudence, avoiding the double trap of anarchy and immobilism. Like fragments of a huge tapestry in movement, with lines that crumble and reform.

The family is coming back, but in a different place: united by affection alone, it claims to be in the service of those who compose it and compatible with the full development of each individual, whether an adult or a child. A significant fact: parents now receive the boyfriends or girlfriends of their children and allow them to spend the night in their homes, something that was unthinkable in the 1970s and 1980s. The concern to remain a solid unit prevails over conventions. The family makes us a link in a long chain that has preceded us and will survive us. It accustoms us to a kind of juxtaposition of young and old in an age when each generation considers itself a nation apart, when adolescents and senior citizens isolate themselves among their peers to forge their own rituals. Open and hospitable, the family now seeks to reconcile two values that used to be irreducible—independence and security—and it asks us to refound on the basis of free choice what was previously imposed on us by birth and by chance. Each of us does what he wants while respecting a common code, and the social safety net is there for everyone.

Baroque Procreations

Today, we choose to have children rather than having them imposed on us: there is nothing more enigmatic than the desire to have children, which is our last form of the sacred. A baby is no longer a matter of chance but a willed result. The couple decides when it wants to conceive, and contraception suspends the anonymous force of instinct: what is natural is to make love, and what is artificial is to give life to a child. An entirely programmed birth is a crushing responsibility: until our dying day, we will be accountable for this person who comes into the world! We have children for all kinds of bad reasons—to reassure ourselves, to survive ourselves, to succeed through them where we have failed. But we love them for better reasons: by simply existing, they upset our narcissistic projections, constantly defeat our expectations. The miracle of the newborn who immediately and continually surprises us: she confirms nothing, she disconcerts, incarnates alterity. Each individual, thinking he is working for his own happiness, in fact labors for the renewal of humanity. In this dialectic of particular intentions and general ends, the height of egoism is also the height of altruism. For our children, we agree to make sacrifices that will never be rewarded. They constitute our last carnal homeland, for which we are prepared to give our lives.

Similarly, blended families entail multiple duties, because one is also responsible for the children of the new spouse—those whom the French call, using a new term, "quasis," sons or daughters who live under the same roof without having any blood ties between them—running the constant risk of misunderstanding. Science and our mentalities now permit us genuine temporal reversals: elderly fathers having a last son younger than their own grandchildren; mothers bearing the children of their daughters and sons-in-law; virgin young women requesting artificial insemination to avoid any sexual intercourse; rich men deciding to have children all by themselves, without women, the sale of cells or uteruses; the possibility of developing, in a few decades, artificial uteruses—an abyss seems to be opening in front of us that upsets all our points of reference. But that is because we are in the midst of creating new familial forms, and we are experiencing the fear of the

transition and not the fear of the end. Yesterday sexual intercourse was essentially connected with procreation; today
it is no longer inseparable from procreation, and tomorrow
procreation will no longer be inseparable from sexual intercourse, so that the intervention of progenitors will be un-
necessary: hypermodernity is only a return to the sources
of the text of the Gospel, since Mary is the first woman to
have conceived without "sin." Where we thought we saw an
upheaval, we find instead a strange fidelity to our origins.[3]
It is not the family that has disappeared, but rather one of
its forms that dates from the eighteenth century and whose
edges have been gnawed away by these new phratries with
tortuous genealogical labyrinths.

The Fear of the Void

"Families, I hate you! Closed homes; closed doors; posses-
sions jealous of happiness," André Gide said. "Families, I
love you," Luc Ferry rightly replied, celebrating the rising
power of private life.[4] Perhaps we should qualify that: families, I love you, but not all the time. These little human con-
centrations have not lost their ambivalent character: they
are both a refuge and a prison. On the one hand, the joy of
feeling protected, of knowing that somewhere there is an
open door, people prepared to take care of you, to feed you.
The irreplaceable role played by childhood homes that condense so many delicious memories. What is more delicious
than optional get-togethers on holidays? It is as if for an evening or a day these great branching households put all their
energy, all their warmth in the service of each member: a

scattering of affective charges and multiple allegiances that diminish to that extent the weight of a single commitment. Didn't Barack Obama say that family gatherings at his home on Christmas, which bring together relatives from four continents, resemble the UN General Assembly? The miracle of these little groups in which one feels immediately at ease. The possibility of choosing those we prefer, of going to seek from an uncle or a forgotten cousin the complicity that we no longer have with our parents.

On the other hand, the family remains a symbol of imprisonment. It is still the part of life that is inherited and not invented. It sometimes pursues us even to the farthest reaches of the Earth, throwing a lasso around our necks, and the more we deny it the more we reproduce it. Entering into the private world of certain tribes is like lifting a stone under which vermin are swarming: aversions, rancors, settlings of old scores. Even if they look friendly, these are compact blocs closed in upon their secrets. It is always within them that the worst abominations break out: rape, incest, murder.[5] The idea that one descends from these people, shares a patronym with them, is sometimes nauseating. There are other, gentler clans that are mutual admiration societies, in which the outsider is brought in only to serve as a mirror for confirming their splendor. In your eyes we are so beautiful, come back and tell us that again! Family love is incontestable: it often stops at the notary's door, when the will is read, when brothers and sisters, their tears hardly dry, quarrel over who will get the largest sum. (Hence the importance of distributing one's wealth to one's children while they are still young, one way of purging affective relationships of any financial perturbation.)

A Pitiless Happiness

In this area, we have moved from one pathology to another: we used to feel imprisoned in the parental enclosure, now we feel abandoned. In the Victorian period, the British philosopher Isaiah Berlin saw the triumph of claustrophobia: captivity and pettiness. For our own time, he foresaw the opposite malady: agoraphobia. The fear of an ocean without dikes or direction. An excessive autonomy would leave us in an affective desert, deprived of any guard rail; the burden of any supervision would overwhelm us. To tell the truth, we would like both, without the drawbacks of either: solidarity without dependency, the bond without the leash. We want the family to be there for us without being there for it, we want it to comfort us, if necessary, but otherwise forget us.

What holds together the members of the same family line? Inclination, shared interests, perhaps, but certainly no longer authority. Nothing prevents the parents from separating, the children from leaving home when they are still adolescents, brothers and sisters from no longer seeing each other. Biology still counts, but by itself it no longer suffices as the basis for a duty. Centered on the happiness of its members, the modern family seeks to be a shelter and a springboard for the child, to give him the necessary protection, to prepare him for the world, to emancipate him. But at the first hitch, couples explode, and the little boy or girl, awkwardly bears witness to a desire that no longer exists, while at the other extremity the elderly are pushed toward the exit and parked in retirement homes. A pitiless happiness that requires some people to make sacrifices. We would like to be able to cancel our leases at will, erase our progeny or our grandparents with a click of the mouse. Consider, for example, Virginia Woolf's magnificent sentence: "No one has the right to block another human being's view." In it, we hear the irresistible call for liberation from the patriarchal or conjugal order. But what if the obstacle in question is a child who has become a burden, a miniature jailer who restricts our aspiration to a larger life? The miraculous synthesis between care for oneself and care for others does not take place: the choices are agonizing and we waver between several dead ends. The family will always be too coercive to meet our need for freedom and not sufficiently present to meet our need for consolation.

There is more: in its triangular form, the one that arose at the end of the eighteenth century and has recently fallen apart, the family group was subject to the command of the all-powerful father, whose whims, to adopt Sartre's phrase, had the force of law. The present-day family speaks only the language of affection: every confrontation is forbidden, every coolness denounced. Only a fusion in which personalities are abolished prevails. Until we become adults, we are supposed to remain little chicks huddling in the nest. The rhetoric of intimacy overflows into society, and in the French media the austere terms *père* and *mère* have been abandoned in favor of *papa* and *maman*. An insipid rhetoric has invaded the public sphere and imposed government in accord with the rules of immediate proximity.[6] Love flaunted prohibits conflict, immobilizes children in a primordial mire that prevents them from rebelling against their parents, who deny themselves any remonstrance in order to avoid destroying the relationship. An octopus-like family that strangles its members by blackmailing them with tenderness. How can one revolt against an avalanche of cuddles and kisses? The supremacy of fathers who are pals and mothers who are girlfriends and dress like their daughters, negating any difference between generations and offering their children only an ultra-permissive credo: do as you wish. "The birth of children is the death of the parents," Hegel said; today, it is instead a way for the latter to remain children until late in life. It forgets that confrontation shapes people, that attachment is not incompatible with opposition, that every age group arises by symbolically murdering the preceding one.[7] And it is the tragedy of people who have been brought up in a way that is too liberal, without prohibitions or supervision, not to have really been brought up. Whence the demand for order, often noted among the children of baby-boomers insisting that their fathers and mothers, eternal Peter Pans, finally assume their responsibilities. Love was supposed to solve everything; it has become part of the problem.

Passionate Ordinariness

Lichtenberg's witty aphorism "Love is blind, marriage restores its sight" is no longer completely true: in our current idylls, affective bewitchment often cohabits with the scruples of lawyers circumscribing their respective territories, dividing up chests and armoires, separating mine from thine. Lovebirds are also economic actors with almost equal footing who enter into life together by delimiting very precise enclaves, having for example a separate bedroom so as not to have to put up with the other's snoring, his insomnias (sleep is much more intimate than sex), his inappropriate erotic requests. People may not even live in the same apartment (which presupposes a certain affluence), thus sparing themselves the constraints of cohabitation, and practicing an intelligent utopia of distance. It would be a mistake to see in all this merely a decline into crude materialism. Today, people are prudent from the outset, so great is the fear of being devoured. To guard one's vital space is to protect oneself from being suffocated, to prevent domestic details from becoming parasitic on the universe of affects. In schools of fish, it seems, the closer their bodies are, the less the fish reproduce. Living on top of each other apparently deprives them of the desire to spawn. Similarly, the best accord is one that avoids symbiosis: if absence puts an end to fleeting infatuations, excessive presence kills the strongest passions. Lovers die from being too close, because they lack the proper interval for communicating with each other. The typical image of the contemporary couple: two persons entwined in the street or sitting at a table in a restaurant, while each uses a cell phone to conduct a conversation with a third party. The delight of being together and separated. But if a conversation goes on too long, the equilibrium is broken. An assiduity based on distance, a proximity obtained by being apart: the lovers teeter on this narrow crest from which they can fall at any moment.

Life together is less solitude surmounted than companionship interrupted. Even the most solidly united couples lead double or triple lives, especially when they both work, and adultery is only one of countless ways of being elsewhere. Spouses must be neither too distant nor too close: they leave the better to come back, and remain in contact by telephone or e-mail. The couple is often on the brink of breaking up over problems of shopping, socks left on the floor, tables not cleared, beds left unmade. To become close friends with a couple is often to be disillusioned, to discover the details of a pettiness that seems unfathomable, so vast is the gap between the image of themselves that they present and what they are in reality. The couple is a little principality that votes its own laws and is constantly in danger of falling into despotism or anarchy. Lovers are simultaneously sovereigns, diplomats, parliament, and people, all by themselves. Perpetual adjustments, frictions avoided, the distribution of household tasks (most of which still fall upon women): the contemporary couple is a very particular conjunction of passion and the stewpot. Even sex becomes a discussion session in which people exchange grievances and suggestions. We ask the other to reassure and surprise us, to make the home both a soft barrier against the world and the site of emotional excitement. Whence the necessity of drawing up a constitution that can be revised at any time and allows each person to find her place and her rhythm. A lack of flair? No doubt, but why must all our loves be heroic? It suffices that they exist: let us cease to seek an excuse for them in passion, fidelity, ardor. We have to choose between glory and permanence.

The Couple as a Happy Conversation

Not all relationships melt like snow in the sun; some last and they're not just the exceptions. In the conflict between gushing forth and wearing away, the lovers have chosen permanence. Their relationship has sometimes been on the skids, they have gone through dark periods, carried away by the muddy waters of depression, have left each other, have overcome these wounds. In the delicate combination of incandescence and duration, they have opted for the latter, which reduces fervor but strengthens confidence. They have chosen the framework of a long-term chronology over the brief flare of desire, but they are also surprised to find that getting used to each other has not completely killed the effervescence, they thank each other for not leaving. This noble perseverance of old couples deserves our attention even if we cannot all follow their example. How can we slow the inevitable erosion of a marriage based on love? By basing the relationship on bonds other than ecstasy and frenzy: on esteem, on complicity, on transmission, the joy of founding a family, the quest, of which the Ancients speak, for a certain immortality through children and grandchildren. We have to rehabilitate the temperate climates of sentiment, oppose to mad love the gentle love that works to build the world, comes to terms with the passing days, sees them as allies, not as enemies.

Happiness, said Mme de Sévigné, is being with those one loves. The happiest outcome of a marriage or of a relationship, is friendship between its members: friendship, that is, passion in slow motion, passion that escapes the pathos of symbiosis, resists separation, and admits the plurality of attachments. It means the acceptance of forms of cohabitation other than those of ardor and intensity, though this excludes neither a return of strong feeling nor enthusiasm in matters of the flesh. A good marriage, said Milton in the seventeenth century, "is a meet and happy conversation."

An admirable definition on condition that the conversation be suspended from time to time without damaging the relationship in any way. One has to know how to be bored together without blaming the other for the boredom, to enjoy this state as the ultimate proof of savoir-vivre and civility.

If there is no wisdom of love,[8] there may still be wisdom in love when it consents to efface itself, to move into the background, accept its defeat by something greater than it is. True love cares little about love. Our ancestors tried to increase their value on the basis of an arranged marriage; we must accomplish the reverse—we must find mutually agreeable arrangements on the basis of an original passion. A couple that lasts is paradoxically a couple that accepts that it will end, sees itself as a way station in an adventure that continues beyond it. The strength of the couple in love is to be weak and malleable, protected by the very quality that makes it vulnerable. It is imperfect, and therefore endlessly reformable. It remains essentially a promise cast over an abyss of doubt, a wager on longevity, an act of confidence in the fertilizing powers of time. There is a kind of noble tenacity in this long itinerary followed together, full of ambushes, temptations, and discouragements, in which one has chosen, through a unique being, one's servitude and one's beatitude.

Should the Conjugal Bed Be Politicized?

The Freudian Marxists of the 1960s are not the only ones who have yielded to the enticements of putting intimacy in the service of ideology. In reality, all philosophers since Plato have seen in the constitution of a sound and peaceful family the precondition for a strong state. In our day, some conservatives discern in the inconstancy of individuals the possible disintegration of democracy: if the couple is rocked by the muddy waters of divorce, of adultery, and of permissiveness, it will be the whole social order that capsizes. "I find that they [the children of divorced parents] are not as open to the serious study of philosophy and literature as some other students are,"[9] noted Allan Bloom, for example. The American sociologist Christopher Lasch, a brilliant analyst of contemporary narcissism, demanded that the Constitution be amended to prohibit divorce for couples with children as well as abortion. Conversely, Anthony Giddens, a theoretician of the British Labour Party, sees in the transformations of intimacy a kind of microcosm of democracy writ large. The invention of the self, respect for others, autonomy: these virtues have an impact on the public sphere and testify to a new dynamism.[10] One side calls for the reestablishment of stable relationships even at the price of coercion, the other is amazed to see individual caprice coinciding with the direction taken by History.

"No one is a good citizen unless he is a good son, a good father, a good brother, a good friend, a good husband," says article 4 of the declaration of 5 Fructidor, year III of the French Revolution (1791), which consecrates the family as the foundation of the social contract. A profound but terrifying formula, because it subordinates the domestic to the political and establishes the supervision of human passions in the name of the collective interest. The revolutionary leader Saint-Just explained that "divorce is a scandal that soils the dignity of the social contract. . . . The more dissolute private morals are, the more important it is that good and humane laws rigorously oppose their disorder. Virtue must yield nothing to men in particular."[11] There has never been a direct connection between the nature of a regime and the morals it protects. A democracy may be puritanical,

India for example, and a totalitarian regime may encourage licentious behavior, as in Cuba or the former Soviet Union. The morality of a leader, Khomeini for example, is not synonymous with civil gentleness. And so far, the senile frolics of a Berlusconi have not killed the Italian Republic. A sociological illusion: love relationships are read like tea leaves, they must absolutely signify something other than themselves. Instead of taking them as facts, scholars consider them to be positive or negative values. In this domain, it is impossible to follow either the prophets of doom or the heralds of a radiant dawn: love is undecidable and there is no reason for it. What has to be challenged is the mechanical deduction of one from the other. Our societies are neither so sick nor so healthy as people say: they are experimental, that is, limping, and they have to reconcile the volatility of the couple with the necessary stability of descent. An immense and exciting challenge: the perils of freedom are worth more than the comforts of constraint. ■

PART III

The Carnal Wonder

CHAPTER 7

Is There a Sexual Revolution?

I have a look around. One of the guys I met in an orgy two weeks ago in an after-party at the Baths is two meters from me, wedged between two sheds. He turns around. We are face to face. Hi, how are you? We kiss each other on the cheek. I would have preferred a kiss on the mouth, after all, we fucked, so we can do that, but since it was in an orgy, he must think it doesn't count.

GUILLAUME DUSTAN, *Je sors ce soir*

True civilization does not consist in gas, steam, or spiritualism, but in the reduction of the traces of original sin.

CHARLES-PIERRE BAUDELAIRE

In August 1993, the magazine *Elle* offered a test for the summer: are you a slut? What is astonishing about this is not merely the crudeness of the question, but also the enthusiasm of the replies: every single one of the editors and journalists working for this famous weekly responded in the affirmative, taking pride in being a bitch, an initiate like no other, the equivalent of a sign of nobility in erotic games.[1]

Turning the insult around in this way shows us, were it necessary, that we have moved into another world. Formerly hidden, people's sex lives are now to be exhibited. A new snobbism based on sensual pleasure: here, nobody wants to be seen as lacking in knowledge. To page through a certain kind of periodicals published over the last thirty years is to find a strange catechism of debauchery that is no less prescriptive than the earlier one: try out sodomy, a ménage à trois, bisexuality, whips and chains, are you a good lay, do you do lunch-hour fucks?[2] Whereas death remains obscene and concealed, the dirty little sexual secret is put on stage, displayed in the public sphere, and everyone can recount it on television, on radio, on the Internet.

The emancipation of morals has played a strange trick on the people of our time. Far from liberating the joyous effervescence of the instincts, it has merely replaced one dogma with another. Formerly lubricity was supervised or prohibited, now it has become obligatory. The collapse of taboos and women's control over their own bodies has been accompanied by an increase in demand: men have to "perform" on pain of being rejected.

Anxious Shamelessness

In the twentieth century, sexuality used to be celebrated as a tool for transforming the world, and was supposed to bring the human race into a state of quasi-perfection. The ambiguous expression "sexual poverty" was forged on the economic model, an expression that implied a scale of libidinal prosperity: there were rich people and poor people, those who lived and those who survived, those who devoted themselves to the magnificent celebrations of the body and those who had to be content with the beggar's portion. No one wanted to be seen as sexually "poor," even in a boring marriage, even with acceptable service records. Sex has become, just like one's profession, salary, and physical appearance, the outward sign of wealth that people add to their social panoply.[3] A new human type has appeared: the hedonistic ascetic who makes great efforts to arouse his senses in order to stimulate his senses and arrive at felicity. He works hard to produce pleasure and is at the same time greatly tormented: his quest has as its counterpart a permanent insecurity. Like the young therapist who has never had an orgasm (in the Canadian film *Shortbus*, 2006) and spends her time frantically masturbating, what everyone seeks is "The Big O," the big orgasm, which is not debauchery but divine grace, the Holy Grail, the passport to a redeemed humanity.[4] Self-fulfillment has to be deserved, and depends on genuine work on the self: erotic engineering accompanied by a highly moral enterprise of self-improvement.

But there is still a vast distance between what this society says about itself and what it actually experiences: for the past half-century, there has been not one investigation of the sex lives of the French, Americans, Germans, or Spanish that has not shown them to be prey to the same obsessions, the same difficulties: men with erectile problems, women who find it difficult or impossible to achieve orgasm.[5] The Kinsey reports, published in 1948 and 1953, revealed private sexual practices that were not in conformity with moral norms.[6] Current investigations describe us as better behaved than we think we are. We used to be called immodest; now we are seen as braggarts. Our parents lied about their morality; we lie about our immorality. In both cases, there is a gap between what we say and what we do. The malaise in our culture no longer arises, as it did in Freud's time, from the instincts' being crushed by the moral order, but rather from their liberation. When the ideal of self-fulfillment triumphs everywhere, each person compares himself with the norm and struggles to come up to the mark. The end of guilt, the beginning of anxiety. However, sex is still largely confined to the domain of what cannot be acknowledged: either we trumpet it too boastfully to be credible, or we hide it for fear of seeming clumsy in a time when intimacy has become a sport for show-offs.[7]

The Civil Wars of the Libido

It is a pleasure to see a new hedonism spreading through the Western world and facilitating the circulation of bodies; it would be naïve not to relate this development to changes in the market, which, in the name of its self-interest rightly understood, rebels against the moral order. The famous situationist slogan "Live without interruption and enjoy without restrictions" was a consumerist ideal. It claimed to be libertarian; in fact it was advertising. It is in the space of the shopping center, of the Internet, of the television screen, that life flows without interruption, twenty-four hours a day, and I can get my hands on every product, switch from one channel to another, buy and communicate with the whole world. Our love and sex lives presuppose delays, interludes, interruptions, enthusiasms, and in no way resemble the continuous, even surface of the world supermarket. It is not to condemn it to note that hedonism, "the insurrection of life" (Raoul Vaneigem), in whatever form it is served up—Epicurean, anarchist, subversive—has become to a large extent a new conformism that waves the flag of transgression in order to sing the praises of the status quo. Sex used to allow us to combine ecstasy with protest; now it is the surest product of consumer society.

In this case, the liberation of desire takes place under the emblem of a belligerent vainglory: the new Dionysians don the garb of the rioter as if nothing had changed and Victorian morals continued to rage with the same ferocity. They invent mighty adversaries for themselves, throw up little barricades of paper, and sell disobedience by the meter the way a draper sells fabric. Even among the most talented of them, what drum rolls, what roaring cannonades! To listen to them, they are playing not with but against society, against big capital, Judeo-Christian culture. Delectation is a weapon pointed at the world, not a moment of happiness shared with another person. Their libertinism is honey spoiled by bitterness: so many essays on the art of enjoyment have in themselves so little joy and so much rage and rancor! Pleasure, by definition, teaches us nothing; it neither improves nor educates human beings, it gladdens their hearts and that is enough. But for our political commissars, pleasure is not a stroke of luck; it is an order. This is not the first time in history that the cult of the body has returned to us wearing the hideous mask of dogmatism. Someday someone should explain why the avant-gardes, surrealism and situationism among others, degenerated into totalitarian convents, swollen with resentment, generating miniature pontiffs whose obsession was to excommunicate, to curse. The pasteurized, polished universe that Reich and his current disciples promise us would have all the gaiety of a military barracks.

There is more: for the past half-century the erotic field has been structured as a sectarian field. It was with Sade that sexuality was put on equal footing with subversion, because he made of it a weapon to be used against feudalism and religion. All that matters is to follow nature in its excesses and to help oneself to objects of desire, whether they are children or adults, the better to blaspheme against God, nobles, and institutions. Among all the great reformers, the purveyors of carnal felicity are not the least mad: they are the inquisitors of the areas below the belt, they hold the key to your salvation and would rather see you die than fail to adopt their ideas. Evangelists for the queer, dissident feminists, multisexuals, adepts of latex and whips, sex performers, virilists bent on revenge, aggressive monogamists, homophobes and heterophobes, priests of the orgasm: so many new coteries that deify their sexual preferences by insulting themselves.[8]

The "maniacs of desire" (Christophe Bourseiller) are first of all maniacs of classification who imprison themselves in the ghetto of their particularity in order to launch fierce attacks on the rest of humanity. All those who condemn the false divisions imposed by nature, machismo, the church, and the bourgeoisie are themselves caught up in the narcissism of small differences and never cease to vituperate against anyone who diverges from their opinion. The rejection of any category takes the form of a new categorization—transgendered people, for example—which reproduces the assignment they rejected. The virulence of social struggles is transferred—an error imported from North America—to struggles about sexual identity: for example, in France some women want to be known as a "Fem" and not a "femme," in order to avoid being reduced to their sex by the established order![9] Here, revolution is a matter of a different way of writing. A whole generation is squandering its energy on this pathetic nonsense. People display their private lives loud and clear through pressure groups, they claim to be militants for their own desire (which closely resembles that of everyone else), the better to denigrate the desire of others. The more they resemble one another, the more they detest one another, and then they exist only by opposing each other. Even "coming out," when it is done in the name of an ideology of truth, has something of a police procedure about it. An irrepressible challenge that excludes any indecision. One has to say what one is and too bad for those who don't know, who don't mind being put in a particular pigeonhole.

A strange outcome for a liberation that ends in aggression: ukases rain down and destroy! Make love not war, they said in the 1960s. To make love today is to start the war of all against all. The idea that joy might come from the collision of epidermises has evaporated. Sex is no longer an activity, it is a stick used to beat others.

Obscenity Is a Long Game of Patience

In a passage in *The City of God*, St. Augustine describes a man's untimely erection as a rebellion of the organs analogous to that of men, after the Fall: "Sometimes this lust importunes them in spite of themselves, and sometimes fails them when they desire to feel it, so that though lust rages in the mind, it stirs not in the body. Thus, strangely enough, this emotion not only fails to obey the legitimate desire to beget offspring, but also refuses to serve lascivious lust; and though it often opposes its whole combined energy to the soul that resists it, sometimes it is also divided against itself, and while it moves the soul, leaves the body unmoved."[10] Augustine imagines Adam and Eve's copulations in the earthly Paradise before the original sin and invents what might be called a sexuality without libido. The first couple are supposed to have conceived in all innocence, and the fruits of their flesh multiplied: "The man, then, would have sown the seed, and the woman received it, as need required." Our ancestors are supposed to have moved their organs as we move our hands or feet, at their leisure. Adam moved at will the parts of the body that are "composed of slack and soft nerves" and that we can "stretch out" or "contract and stiffen."[11] In other words, united by the bond of a chaste love for his spouse, Adam is supposed to have, contrary to Pierre Brassens's song,[12] controlled his member without difficulty. A mechanical act, cleansed of all emotional charge: Augustine seems to have anticipated today's pornography, with its deenergized sexuality.[13]

The erotic image, hidden in a world of taboos, used to offer people the spectacle of actual nudity, allowing them to contemplate the dreadful mystery. Anyone who lived through the legalization of X-rated films and images in the 1970s knows what was going on: the explicit representation of the female genitals was staggering for the novice spectator. Since that time, we've gotten used to it; the forbidden areas of our bodies have lost part of their secret, at least on the screen. Porno is a utopia that we mistake for reporting, or even for an educational project. Many people consider it a kind of primary school of strong emotions that answers the question: what to do? But it does not reflect reality, it stylizes it, and limits itself to filming automatons. That is why it may intimidate young people who are incapable of equaling the performances of these male or female athletes.

Like a horror film, it is doomed to follow a strategy of outdoing: one has to astonish the spectator even if it means falling into cheap tricks (as in François Reichenbach's 1976 film *Sex O'Clock*, in which a man pulls a chain out of his anus). The camera explores the inside of the body, becomes a kind of endoscopy, a gynecological examination: everything is shown, but nothing is visible. The effort to open our eyes ends up blinding us. Hardcore pornography ends up being a kind of gymnastics, plays crudely with organic substances—blood, sperm, urine—and ends up parodying itself, defusing itself. For it to retain its effectiveness, its producers would have to move beyond easy ways of making money and have the audacity to follow the example of horror films, in which not allowing the viewer to see everything increases her anxiety. The sole question professional pornographers should ask is how to make impropriety keep its promises. But pornography may be doomed, by its very nature, to be a genre that produces a certain ambiance, like the canned music played in elevators and parking lots.

Pornography's real crime is its mediocrity and the fact that it always ends up with the same genital or anal acrobatics, and this is also true of its feminist versions, which are decorated with a politico-militant discourse that is as pedantic as it is hollow. When in order to transform "dominant males into interchangeable cocks," Annabel Chong engaged, in 1999, in the largest gang-bang in the world (251 partners in twelve hours), she did not overturn any dominant code, but merely added another chapter to the Guinness Book of World Records.[14] At a time when any teenager, evading parental supervision, can see dozens of scabrous sites on the Internet, competition to produce excitation is intense, and for Eros the end of clandestinity is also the end of a certain attraction. Sex has ceased to be a sensational event that throws minds into turmoil, and now seems to be an old-fashioned audacity that the recent liberalization of mores has condemned us to experience as a cliché.

However, that is clearly not the case, because sexuality still has a powerful influence that we cannot control. In a certain sense, everything has already been seen, and nothing is experienced; we might even say that adolescents' appetite for erotic images, a phenomenon that has been present in every period, correlates with a total ignorance of love—an immense erudition accompanied by a crude misunderstanding. Linguistic enthusiasm against the background of obscenity is typical of young men who are virgins. There are lexically precocious words that are libidinal dawns. In certain milieus, the macho regression encouraged by tradition coexists with pornography, or at least it is expressed in that language; in this respect, the aggressive misogyny of the riff-raff in the slums has infected the fashionable neighborhoods, when twelve- or thirteen-year-old girls are called dirty whores and sluts as they emerge from the school building. Scorn for women draws on an X-rated vocabulary. The fall of prohibitions seems also to have contributed to the depreciation of the objects of desire. Porn tends to transform obscenity into a cliché: a decline in the rate of excitation, a rise in the rate of saturation. The most outrageous positions, the crudest expressions do not long remain and go stale like a wine that has been open too long. The vulgarity of a certain sexual lexicon, which has entered into ordinary language, ends by seizing up and sinking into kitsch. A dreary, mass-produced shamelessness that loses in intensity what it gains in extension.

Thus chic pornography markets provocation; major brands go slumming by combining luxury with lechery and flirting with taboos in order to get a rise out of a market on the verge of saturation. A performer like Madonna seems to have exhausted this vulgar symbolism, groping her crotch on stage, combining Christ and the dildo, giving French kisses to the members of her band, invoking the whole imaginary world of the orgy and S&M, all for the benefit of the suckers applauding her. Pornography is the best antidote for the images it disseminates: it transforms infraction into routine. It should be prescribed as a remedy for insomnia: its soporific powers are enormous! In the end, its problem is that it is coitus by proxy: I am not involved. That is why so many doughty citizens make amateur pornographic films. These men display erections worthy of Sardanapalus, produce multiple geysers of seminal fluid, whereas their wives, spangled with sperm, caress themselves with vibrators (no doubt running on solar energy, as ecological awareness requires). Just as there are philosophers who sell wisdom in kit form, these amateurs cobble together their pocket pornography at home as a kind of do-it-yourself project.

Ultimately, the real obscenity is our eagerness to contemplate the death and suffering of others, our taste for catastrophes on television or on the highway, when everyone
stops to look at the mangled bodies after an accident. The
crowds that used to hasten to witness executions were not
moved by a concern for justice: by taking pleasure in the
agony of people they did not know, they sought to conjure
the horror of death. Staring at these tormented beings, they
were both disgusted and calmed.

A Little Reserve, Please

The end of prohibitions about thirty years ago has probably produced too many laboriously unbridled narratives
that omit no posture, no description—to the point that we
are grateful to writers and film-makers who avoid smutty
scenes in their works. We thank them for sparing us the
endless acrobatics, ecstasies, and groans.

Some people still long for the time when loving was synonymous with taking a risk: censorship was able to make
precious that of which it deprived us. Its resistance to our
desires functioned as an obstacle and as an auxiliary: someone who transgresses is begging for divine punishment.
There is a great coalition of puritans and pornocrats, the
former conferring on the defiance of the latter the status of
a scandal: artists need the hypocrisies of the moral majority
so that they can declare themselves persecuted, they need
this statue of the Commander in order to raise a few vaguely
licentious bits of trash or scathing pamphlets to the level
of cultural events. If this alliance were to break down, the

result would be panic. The same question arose in the seventeenth and eighteenth centuries. Under the Old Regime, blasphemy had an ambiguous status: it had to be situated in a society characterized by strong religious belief, in which the dogmas in force invited profanation. Saint-Simon described the orgies of the Duke of Orléans, a famous libertine during the Regency: "People drank heavily, got excited, shouted filthy things at the top of their lungs, and tried to outdo each other in impiousness."[15] Even the wild atheism of a writer like Sade still looks like indirect homage to the Church: the countless sacrileges committed by his characters, the little condemnations that get people excited, the profanations of the host or the cross are all ways of reviving God by insulting him. Every degrading discourse is dependent on a taboo that it has to overthrow. The worst injury one can do a scandalous book is to authorize it. How many authors dream of being forbidden in order to enjoy the halo of the accursed?

We can distinguish between at least two kinds of crudeness: a Christian one, that of the penitentials or confession manuals, which awakens desire on the pretext of chastising it, and a modern one, which dries up desire while thinking it is describing it as it is. To condemn illicit practices, ecclesiastical authorities had to name them, at the risk of making them attractive: copulation *a tergo*, pollution with one's hands by rubbing them against a woman's genitals or the buttocks of a boy, fornication with a virgin, a servant, or an animal.[16] Inversely, the proliferation of the salacious in contemporary literature (Bret Easton Ellis and his European epigones) has resulted in a devaluation of sex by representing it as repetitive and ugly. A victory of the erotico-depressive, this mixture of audacity and extreme sadness. Come, fuck, bugger, jack off—this basic vocabulary is not provoking but conventional, stringing together identical sequences. A new academicism of trash that is, fortunately, occasionally saved by humor.[17] Eros is generally voluble and makes us talk too much: is it too much to ask of it that it vary its rhetoric a bit and spare us the constant repetitions? In a few decades, we have moved from famine to satiety.

The great erotic texts are decorous in their shamelessness; they employ understatement to suggest excess. There are brilliant short-circuits that stun us, and omission is often the royal road to transgression. Why eliminate elegance from the domain of the intimate; why try so hard to impress us? Earthiness does not exclude sophistication. Notable in this regard is the move, in the domain of the novel, from the disturbing realism of Jean Genet, Tennessee Williams, Hubert Selby Jr., Tony Duvert, Henry Miller, or Georges Bataille to the sexually correct realism of so many contemporary novelists who write "explicitly" with neither emotion nor grace. The power of language lies in its ambivalence, the slippage of meaning, the implicit, the subtle mixture of aggressiveness and restraint. Crude words are not in themselves exciting; it is the excitement of the moment that makes their use necessary. In the heat of the action, they immerse us in the same sadomasochism, accompanying the act like indispensable ingredients. Out of context, they are incongruous, laughable. What is lacking in too many contemporary books is the dimension of celebration, even in the abject; the fact is that eroticism remains an astounding domain that we cannot get over. Doesn't Jean

Paulhan speak of a "relentless decency" apropos of the *Story of O*? The delights provided by expression: the delight of escaping, through expression, from oppression, but also that of escaping from drivel, from the standard stereotype of debauchery. The more language rids itself of its complexes, the more it impoverishes itself and the more glacial it becomes.

Is the Libido a Recreational Activity?

It is as if we had liberated sex at the price of extinguishing desire, as if sex had liberated itself from us. A half-century-long cycle is closing and leading us, in this area, from repression to depression. A way of making sexuality as inoffensive as a tall glass of water.[18] Modern, "liberated" persons, whether male or female, don't want to hear any nonsense— for them, "sex is fun," it is a natural function, and they practice a libidinal serve-yourself system as a couple or a group, and want to try everything. They organize "fuckerware parties," a vibrator version of Tupperware parties, and cannot get along without their sex toys, accessories as harmless as a teddy bear or an incense candle. Don't worry, be happy: that is its motto. We owe to the Clinton-Lewinsky affair the extraordinary debate, worthy of the Byzantine Empire, as to whether fellatio could be categorized as a friendly act, a proof of comradeship at school and in the office. At what point does the sex act begin? With a kiss, with penetration, with caresses, with mutual masturbation? In the case of some people, it never takes place at all: even fully entangled with each other, they remain completely detached. Others are inflamed by a simple touch of the fingers. We can assume that most people realize it when they enter a state of physical turmoil, carnal excitement. There is something suspect, in its false simplicity, about Western societies' insistence on saying everything, showing everything. There are various ways of freeing oneself from the libido: demonizing it as sin, extinguishing it by asceticism, destroying it by liberating morals, reducing it to a recreational activity.

However, our attitude toward sexuality is never completely relaxed: those who brag about living without taboos still have to invoke them as ghosts. Our sexuality needs their intoxicating nearness in order to spice up an act that would otherwise be in danger of becoming monotonous. Taboos do not disappear; some are frozen and reappear elsewhere in a harder, more intransigent form. We combine two incompatible aspirations, one to ever-increasing emancipation and the other to ever-increasing vigilance against the perverts who threaten our well-being. That is why our liberated age is also an age that fills its prisons with sex offenders.[19] It is as if society were taking revenge for the license granted in matters of morals by punishing mercilessly those who do not take their pleasure in conformity with the rules. Formerly marked with the sign of sin, deviancy is now both medicalized and penalized in a process that involves the psychiatrist, the judge, and the police.[20] The inconsistency of a time that venerates two opposed principles: pleasure for everyone and respect for individual consent.[21]

Perhaps we should see in this penal panic a sign of the difficulty we experience in reconstructing prohibitions by consensus, whereas tradition imposed them on the ancients. To create them, we fabricate guilty persons, at the risk of sometimes accusing the innocent, as the Outreau child abuse trial held in France in 2004 showed.[22] Instead of inventing new norms, we fill our prisons, and after the death of taboos we subject ourselves to the rule of a floating taboo that is all the more severe because it is never defined as such. The panic about security derives from the undecidable nature of our new prescriptions: it is easier to demonize sex offenders than to provide a rational foundation for their frantic incarceration.[23] We expect the law to determine what is licit and what illicit, and we re-create a community of compassion with victims (with a clear fascination in the case of crimes involving children), and this collective repulsion claims by itself to provide the basis for legislation. We resent these "sickies" who have destroyed our idyll, spoiled the promise of a good sexuality capable of reconciling human beings with themselves: they are paying for our lost illusions.

It is as if in this way we were rediscovering what the great religions and psychoanalysis have taught us, namely that sex is neither neutral nor "nice," but two-sided, pleasure and death, light and dark at once, that "Sexuality is one of those primary forces whose sovereignty over man is assured by man's firm belief in his sovereignty over it."[24] The vocabularies of aggression and delectation are the same: *fuck* and *bugger* mean both to cheat and to make love, and all the words related to this act have a violent connotation. Sex is the barbarous, overpowering side of humanity that we can barely civilize or discipline, and it is disquieting because it does not fit into any great narrative, any odyssey of redemption or decline. The life impulse includes death, Thanatos is part of Eros as much as its opposite, and they both construct humans while destroying them. Let us note that AIDS did not reestablish taboos but gave rise to prudence, the use of condoms and a more careful choice of partners. It teaches nothing, it is a terrible and absurd illness such as nature, in its indifference, regularly produces. Sexuality transcends us: it submerges the individual in the great process of renewing the generations, makes it a link in a chain, "the mortal bearer of an immortal substance."[25] Too strong for us, it burns us, ravages us, and we are never equal to the inhuman demand that it makes on us. Thus a revolution is impossible, if by that we mean that we will someday resolve the question of sex, unless we take the word *revolution* literally, as referring to a periodic rotation like that of a planet in its orbit. In this domain, we always return to the point of departure, we never know anything.

The Empire of the Bimbo

The bourgeoisie and the whore used to have well-defined roles: the decorous and acceptable fell to the former, the vulgar and the garish to the latter. But the Second Empire in France was haunted by a confusion of codes, a gradual gangrene of the social body that emerged from the lower depths: the idea that a tart might resemble a decent middle-class woman terrified people. This distinction has been redistributed differently in our time: a streetwalker is often chic and austere, while soccer moms like to dress like whores. Thus for the last two decades we have seen women and girls baring their anatomies, emphasizing their breasts and buttocks, letting their g-strings stick out of their jeans, in short, making themselves look like porn stars with a disarming naïveté. A transfer of symbols: the uniform of the venal professions becomes that of the ordinary woman.

Disguised as a loose woman, with her body trussed up and her figure highlighted to excess, the latter establishes the world-wide hegemony of the whore.

It is curious that women, having won their independence, should thus present themselves as objects of desire. Why flaunt one's libidinal patrimony in public? In order to escape anonymity, but especially in order to say: "I'm hot, so far as sensual promises go, you'll never find me lacking." The whore combines the two models of the adolescent and the tease, youth and expertise. She suggests sexual skill, a radiant lustfulness. The whores' international has its own icons: Britney Spears, Paris Hilton, Lady Gaga, Victoria Beckham, bare-breasted and futile minxes representing a subculture of aggressive femininity. This eccentric flaunting has to be understood as uncertainty about gender. The play on clichés is no less striking among males: Rambo, Terminator, and all the stars bulked up on steroids are symptoms of an age that no longer believes in virility and has to go to excess in the size of the biceps and the volume of the pectorals. Like the glorification of primitive machismo among some gays, the obsession with hard, enormous cocks and men dressed in policemen's or neo-Nazi outfits, covered with chains and wearing military caps, have a parodic dimension. The huge bodybuilders wearing extremely form-fitting pants that are open in front and in back are not disguised SS-men but actors who snare virility in its very signs. The whore, the neo-macho, the transvestite, the drag queen, and the butch lesbian all thrive on this mixing up of roles.

It would be a mistake to think that the whore has fallen into the madness of a Messalina. Just as women used not to be quite so decent as they seemed to be, the shockingly decked out women of today are not as savvy as we think. "Let us imagine," Georges Bataille says, "the surprise of someone who (by machination) witnesses, without being seen, the sexual transports of a woman whom he had

regarded as particularly distinguished. He would see an illness. The analogue of rabies in dogs. As if some bitch in
heat had substituted itself for the personality of the woman
who received him so properly in her drawing room." We
might say the opposite for the whore: under her flaunted
whorishness, there may be a touching modesty, the awkwardness of a prude. Not all loose women are low-lifes.
Above all, they have to capture attention with a sense of
stage-setting, a talent in displaying their charms that demands respect. Large breasts, swollen lips, full buttocks,
various tattoos—allurements that say only one thing: look
at me. The respectable housewife forced to dress like a slut
is a martyr to a period that has made sex the key to human
behavior. The height of mystification: women wearing a veil
and a g-string, seeming to conform to the law of the fathers
and brothers and surreptitiously asserting themselves as
desiring subjects and as seductive. This would be a good
research project: how many wives and female students in
the Arab-Muslim world, and also in our suburban ghet-
tos, play this kind of trick on the rules of their morality? In
any case, the whore is too true to be credible. Her provocation is a way of thumbing her nose at the stereotypes of the
woman-object that she simultaneously renews and defuses.
She makes her body a stage on which clichés flourish and
fade, she dons masks, one over the other, in order not to be
imprisoned by any of them. The indecent is no less enigmatic than the respectable. The new woman may be the
sum of all the figures that have appeared in the course of
history: poisonous beauty and snow queen, perverse vamp
and loving mother, starry-eyed girl and leader of men, depravity and tenderness combined in the same way that the
new masculinities combine all the aspects of virility more
than they move beyond them.

Under the bimbo's bursting bra, a heart is always beating. ■

CHAPTER 8

Toward a Bankruptcy of Eros?

Anyone who offers to free humanity from its
exuberant sexual subjection, no matter what
nonsense he spouts, will be considered a hero.

SIGMUND FREUD, *Letters to Fließ*

Young woman, 35, pretty, prof. success, seeks man
for good times, discussions, companionship. Must be
intelligent and impotent.

GABY HAUPTMANN, *Cherche homme impuissant
pour relation de longue durée*

I also love it when someone goes down on me when
I'm bleeding. It's kind of a test of mettle for the guy.
When he's finished licking and looks up with his
blood-smeared mouth, I kiss him so we both look
like wolves that who've just ripped open a deer.

CHARLOTTE ROCHE, *Wetlands**

A few years ago, I ran into an old friend with whom I used
to go out. A little maliciously, she said: "I hope you, too,
are finished with sex? It was good for the 1980s. Today it's

**Translator's note:* I quote the English translation by Tim Mohr, New York:
Grove, 2010 (reprint), p. 110.

totally without interest." I stupidly protested. This remark
had caught me off guard. For many people, the libido is
far from being a marvelous drive, and is instead a terrible
source of concern that contradicts the modern dream of
the dispassionate individual. To desire is still to suffer, as
Buddhists would say, because it is to aspire to something
one does not have. That is why the liberation of mores takes
two extreme and opposed forms: violence and abstinence,[1]
a mad experimentation on the one hand, and the abandonment of eroticism on the other.

The Exponential Growth of Thrills

There are people, though they are in the minority, who
seek to follow their worst whims, being convinced that
these whims are good in themselves and that one has to
try everything. The first pleasure of deviation being that
of naming things—fist-fucking, caning, golden showers,
voyeurism—one enters into foreign territory by means of
a neologism. Deviance, even mild, is above all a matter of
language. We can laugh at couples who put makeup on each
other, harness each other, tie each other up, and go to orgies
the way their parents went to mass, descend to the bizarre
and exotic in order to rekindle the flame.[2] Variation reduces
natural coitus to its nature as one possibility among others. The slightest penchant becomes a mode of access to a
special sensual pleasure that is staged, even at the price of
pain or humiliation: an inverted Stoicism that makes each
sensation an adventure of the will. How can we avoid being
reminded of Sade, who wrote: "The wholly selfish man is

one who knows how to transform all distastes into tastes, all repugnances into attractions."

Not just anyone can gain access to any given "perversion": bodies have predispositions that no education can completely erase. Moreover, among the families of Eros, the differences remain enormous: there is no connection between the occasional effusions of a couple who wear masks and buy latex toys on the Internet and the violence of a backroom where unprotected intercourse is carried on, or between a wife who on a lazy Sunday makes herself up as a dominatrix in order to scourge her husband's bottom and the extremism of a performer who lacerates himself, hangs himself from the ceiling from hooks in his breasts, or worse yet, castrates himself in public.[3] Whether one alters one's anatomy to meet surgical or chemical norms, or has oneself tortured, in every case it is a matter of contradicting the body in order to make a constructed body that no longer belongs to one. The flesh starts telling stories other than the eternal genital romance, and the epidermis and the mucous membranes are considered virgin land, a malleable space. We can indignantly reject this culture of bizarre eccentricity, but we cannot deny that it shows a certain megalomania, a morality of the omnipotence of the ego over the instincts: a re-creation of the individual by himself, even if it involves quasi-suicide or mutilation. The goal is to arrive at a point of incandescence where erotic madness can no longer be distinguished from nausea, where distress and sensual pleasure coincide. We can understand the importance these mavericks accord to rituals that discipline pain: the law has been expelled in order to impose the rule, the pact henceforth governs intimate relations. There has to be a code, which can itself be revoked, in order to intensify lust and draw from it, by a rigorous dramatization, the maximum of energy.[4]

There is an exponential growth of thrills in which the escalation ideally has no limit other than death, in which love becomes the odyssey of controlled excess. A veritable fictional sex, since new surfaces for pleasure are forged for the senses, sometimes with the aid of drugs. A transgression of limits in the name of the following principle: I am my body, I have a body, I make myself another body. All the more so because in the age of AIDS nonpenetrative forms of sexuality combine paroxysm and hygiene, and permit exhilaration without contamination. The rejection of natural processes, the taste for privation—where have we already seen that in our history? Who is it that endured physical abuse and famine in the name of another world? The Christian ascetic, of course. From the Desert Fathers to the Catholic saints who subjected themselves to the most painful mortifications (such as licking the wounds of plague victims), the goal was to humble the flesh in order to hasten the advent of a glorious body[5] and to associate oneself with the invisible order of God. To escape from matter was to escape the perishable, and according to St. Ambrose sexuality was the fatal scar that separated us from the perfection of Christ.[6] What if we found at the heart of the most radical acts of our profane universe the religious experience that is at the source of Western culture? That would once again verify Chesterton's brilliant intuition that "The modern world is full of Christian ideas gone mad." The supreme culmination of sexual liberation is the abandonment of sex in favor of high intensities of suffering and repulsion overcome.

The New Defrocked Priests of Sensual Pleasure

The rebellion against biological fatalism is also marked by the return of a notion that we had thought abolished, namely continence, which has been reclaimed by new minorities. This development would have delighted the French utopian Charles Fourier, who would have accorded these dissidents a place of honor in his system, as exceptions to the rule. From the outset, we have to draw a distinction here: the old abstinence was obligatory, the new is voluntary (leaving aside the chastity resulting from surfeit between old married couples who know each other by heart). The former fulfilled various functions: silencing the body's animal needs, combining fasting with carnal abstinence, putting an end to the immodesty of both the genitals and the mouth in order to purify the soul.[7] To refine the analysis, one could say that the ancients aspired to a wise management of the body, whereas Christians sought to transform it in order to wrench it away from the animal world and have done with procreation. In the words of Clement of Alexandria, the goal was not to moderate one's desire but to abstain from desire itself.[8] Virginity was not only a state undergone but also a chosen conquest. One was not born a virgin, one became a virgin by rejecting the corruption of this world and substituting for the purity of the body, an attribute of young women, a perpetual and irrevocable purity of soul open to both sexes.

Today, chastity is instead a reaction to the obligation to achieve orgasm that is hammered into us day and night. Hedonism, which used to be subversive, has become the norm, and now it is the old norm, self-control, that has become subversive. And since we have to pay daily tribute to those new divinities, happiness and self-fulfillment, why should we be surprised to find that many young people are deciding not to do sexual forced labor?[9] Moreover, we are wrong to assume that everyone has a sexuality; some people have none, and don't miss it.[10] (How many adolescents "fuck to be polite," to conform to dominant conventions?) Voluntary hibernation is chosen to escape conformism, to open oneself to other kinds of treasures that the genital obsession conceals from us. Rejecting the sensual diktat is a way of showing dissidence and makes it possible to approach the most essential goods. (For men, we must also emphasize the fear of losing vital energy, the concern to economize their resources. The caste of those who renounce sex is in this case a caste of savers.)

Let there be no mistake: this lack of sexual appetite is still defined in relation to the established order. We are far from the third-century monk Origen who, with a striking sense for the shortcut, castrated himself in order to arrive more quickly at his paradise; nor does this lack of appetite have anything in common with the continence of most of our great philosophers—Kant, Kierkegaard, Nietzsche—who were conceptual virgins, frustrated bachelors, and ferocious misogynists, living the ascetic ideal in their own flesh, even while claiming they were combating it, imposing silence on their bodies the better to serve thought.[11] Nothing indicates that the emphasis laid on "purity " by some North American Christians who required their future spouses to save themselves for the wedding night, and even to avoid shaking hands, is not a trick played by desire that defers consummation in order not to die immediately.

"True love waits," said for example a movement founded by a pastor in Nashville in the mid-1990s: "Because girls are roses, each time they engage in sexual relations before marriage they tear off one of their pretty petals."[12] Again, still in America, consider the "purity ball," which has a strong incestuous connotation, and in which little girls, sometimes as young as nine, take an oath, in the presence of their fathers, to remain virgins until they marry, whereas the father promises not to cheat on his daughter's mother and to keep his soul pure![13] There are even wives who have their hymens surgically repaired in order to rejuvenate themselves and rediscover the thrill of "a second first time." We also find the notion of "Secondary Virgins": a girl who has lost her virginity in a moment of weakness is given a second chance provided that she swears an oath, in the presence of her friends, not to do it again. Sex cannot be sullied; it must be the consequence and not the premise of marriage. If flirting is permissible, that is because it makes it possible to test one's self-control and to know how far one can go and no farther. A moral and sanitary prophylaxis that makes physical integrity the guarantee of a sentiment's authenticity. Venereal haste reduces marriage to the rank of an experiment and deprives it of its sacred character.

We find the same obsession with virginity among certain Europeans of Muslim origin who combine two models, the consumerist and the traditionalist. For example, a young man from the suburban slums of Paris declared: "When I go to a car dealer, I don't expect to be sold a used car at the price of a new one," explaining that he makes love with girls in his neighborhood but to get married and please his parents, he will go find a virgin in his village. As a use-value, a wife has to be an object that has never been used, and as a symbolic value, her "purity" shows an allegiance to the customs of the culture of origin.[14] A double regression that reminds us, at least in its economic aspect, of rural mores in early modern Europe, in which a cow was more valuable than a wife, the latter being easily replaceable, especially if her successor brought with her a little money and a few pieces of furniture.[15]

The Terror of Disaffection

The ideal of self-control before marriage involves a process of paradoxical eroticization that reminds us of the ritual of initiation in the work of the troubadours, the *assaï*. This was composed of several degrees: attending the lady's rising and going to bed, contemplating her gradual denudation, seeing her body as a microcosm of nature, with its valleys and hills, and finally getting into her bed and engaging in various caresses without going all the way.[16] This long peregrination tended to glorify the burning of desire in order to bring it to its acme. Delaying satisfaction, multiplying obstacles in order to sublimate the appetites: that may be what modern-day fanatics of chastity are reviving without knowing it. The *mezza voce* return of asceticism might be only a stratagem used by the libido to get itself going again: a strange telescoping of two adversaries, asceticism reinventing precious prohibitions in order to generate precious delights.

In our time, what is truly feared is not turpitude but purely and simply the bankruptcy of Eros. How many men retreat before the demands of their companions, claiming in their turn to have a headache, faking orgasm in order to get it over with more quickly, and how many women give up out of weariness? In Europe, we have a heroic image of desire, a torrent that carries everything with it and against which we have to build dikes. The ancient Japanese, who were wiser, represented desire as a "floating world" without anchorage, incarnated by the courtesans in boats who awaited travelers on the rivers.[17] Water as a metaphor of desire: undulation and instability. Nothing can slow it, but a trifle can halt it. It is inconstant even in its inconstancy; it is not insatiable, it is volatile. Against this danger of bankruptcy, reinforcements of the old prudery are not too much to raise the stakes.

What is puritanism? The bourgeoisie's last form of heroism, according to Max Weber, but also a machine for exacerbating sexuality by challenging it. (North America is a good example of this.) In this sense, it is a case of the paradox Hegel described: the better to free himself from the flesh, the Christian who renounces it has to think about it all the time. The tiniest tremor of the senses frightens and immobilizes him, and in spite of himself he makes it his life's central experience.[18] Restraining the flesh's incontinence is a way of leaving a bonfire at the heart of humanity, the better to be consumed by it. The procedure lacks finesse but not efficiency. The hidden goal of this repression is to prevent "erotic entropy" (Sloterdijk), to keep humans from yielding to disenchantment. To maintain prohibitions is to make sensual desire permanent on the condition that the tension is relieved, at regular intervals, through a good collective infraction. In this sense, the tortures inflicted on Iraqi prisoners at Abu Ghraib by the Pentagon's non-coms, which included being forced to take off their clothes and simulate sodomy or fellatio, are a precise version of American puritanism. A nation whose sexuality has made it sick cannot help visiting its neuroses upon the peoples it subjugates. The zeal Sergeant Lynndie England showed in these tortures also proves that women, when put in positions of power, can be just as barbarous as men. License and abstinence rediscover their immemorial pact, and desire draws new youth from being forced into the background. In any event, the pantheon of love is enriched by two new figures: the virgin volunteer and the militant eunuch.

The Metaphysics of the Penis

Julien Carette, a French actor who had grown old, one day shouted to his wife from the second floor of their house:

"Laurence, come quick! I've got a hard-on!"

"Come down," his wife said, "I'm in the garden."

"No, come up, it won't survive the trip!"

The anecdote is symptomatic. It proves, contrary to our prejudices, that men are the weaker sex. Male sexuality is in fact characterized by two complementary phenomena: bad timing and rarity. What does a teenage boy learn upon entering the world of sexuality? To restrain himself as much as possible, that is, to resist nature. Otherwise, the sex act would last hardly more than a few seconds, sperm, like blood, being too quick to flow. Premature ejaculation does not require any maturation. It carries off all the male's vigor, and he finds himself deprived of his pleasure itself for a shorter or longer time, depending on his age. If his penis is slow in hardening, he will be angry with himself for having run out of steam too soon. The male penis: a capricious animal that rises up when it is not wanted, a phoenix that appears and disappears like an indocile servant, either too present or too absent.

A Greek myth that ought to be taught in every school tells us that during an argument between Hera and Zeus, the latter, against his wife's opinion, maintained that women feel more pleasure in love than men do. To settle the dispute, Hera called in Tiresias, whom she had transformed into a woman for seven years as punishment for killing two serpents. Tiresias responded: "If in love pleasure were divided into ten parts, women would have three times three and men only one." Exasperated, Hera struck Tiresias blind, but Zeus granted him the gift of divination, and also made him capable of living seven times seven lives. This legend says it all about the male handicap (to which we must add man's inability to bear children).

The supreme joy for man involves such a loss of energy that it is comparable to death. Because nature made him capable of reproduction, his sexuality is functional, and dies insofar as it fulfills itself. Masculine eroticism is only a series of ruses for circumventing the final emission: in ancient China as in tantric Hinduism, the wise man was advised never to spill his seed and to draw women's power in through his penis. Man must instrumentalize himself in order to endure, to make his sex organ a prosthesis: his first dildo is his penis.

This explains the fascination mixed with envy exercised on men by the clitoris, that "kindling that ignites the great fire of orgasm" (G. Zwang), which is hidden in the folds of the female body and vies with the penis: an unfair competition, since it seems able to have endless orgasms and lead women into unimaginable delights. That also explains the boy's overinvestment in the genital and the fact that many men describe their sexual performance in quantitative terms. They are only keeping at bay the precarious nature of their tools, and the impudent Hercules who are infatuated with themselves are children whining about the simplicity of male sexuality. Every man has known at least once in his life one of the breakdowns that Stendhal called fiascoes. If male sexuality is worried about itself, that is because for men as well, anatomy is fate. Woe to the impotent man: he suffers from not being able to escape himself. His infirmity cuts him off from the community of the living, and we know that the resulting pain can drive men to suicide. (It has been suggested that impotence was what drove Romain Gary and Hemingway to kill themselves.) Instead of desiring a person, he desires desire, fetishizes his sex organ, and ends up no longer caring about anything but it, provoking the failure that it seeks to avoid. Immured in himself, he can no longer rejoin the beloved. Everything that reinvigorates the recalcitrant member is welcome: the immense progress made thanks to Viagra makes it possible to deprive this pathology of its fatality.

What is an erection? A state of potential connection, a call for contact, a bridge to the other. In it, there is something like the exhilaration of a radiant power, an aspiration to invade the other, to merge with the other. It alone offers us this oceanic feeling of being at one with the other, and opens up to us from within the fascinating territories of the other's pleasure. The intoxicating feeling of being initiated into mystery that will always be beyond our understanding.

It is wrong to scorn the mechanical side of the sex act, as Fellini did apropos of Casanova, whom he caricatured as a human piston pounding away at the flanks of the infinite. "Love has no importance," said Alfred Jarry, "since it can be repeated indefinitely." The inverse is true: repetition alone is the foundation of the beauty of the carnal act. It is from the automatic that the spark is born; these reiterated gestures are necessary for the new to emerge. That is why love is also a repertoried choreography that one has to have internalized when one was young in order to forget it later on, the way the hand of the craftsman, painter, or musician does its work without his thinking about it. Men and women have to make themselves into machines, the better to lose their heads; sometimes bodies become robotic, reproduce mindless pantomimes, and become, as Plato said, the spectators of the other's pleasure. In intercourse, an anonymous force bears us, on which we lean, lulled to the point of hypnosis by the reproduction of the same movements. The joy of sensing one's strength, feeling one's organism to be an ally that will never fail us.

The Vertigo of Annihilation

There are two kinds of love: the exclusive, which is more common and unites two persons, and the multiple, which is rare and brings together in a single impulse a large group of individuals. It is the very principle of charity to be "undetermined" (Simone Weil) and to reject preference in order to include the whole of suffering humanity. The fact that a small number of people devote themselves body and soul to those in need, without knowing them, deploying admirable reserves of generosity, is in itself extraordinary. These people proceed on the basis of a "holy indifference" (Francis de Sales) that puts all the afflicted on the same level. As they use it, the word *indifference*, which also signifies hardheartedness, indolence, or ataraxy, becomes the expression of generosity itself: indifference to reward or hardship, a pure abnegation that cares not at all about recompense, "claims nothing, expects nothing, desires nothing" (Mme Guyon).[19] The same bond connects, without fusing them, altruism, venality, and loving hospitality, which all value the multitude. The devotion of a humanitarian to the disadvantaged and the "road to the annihilation of the self" in God seem to have nothing in common with the pleasure of forgetting oneself in a collective erotic convulsion. Except the same taste for the indistinct, the same will to belong to everyone without belonging to anyone. "I could be anyone," writes the American novelist John Richy, telling how he allows himself to be taken by shadowy figures met at night in public parks, and who jump him without saying a word.[20] In eroticism there is a sensual pleasure in dissolution. Do with me what you will. The joy of disappearing into the other, of losing oneself in a nameless, faceless crowd, of being seized by hands and mouths, of keeling over at the slightest touch. The "glory hole," apparently of Japanese origin, is well-known. It is found in gay bars and some heterosexual peep-shows: a hole pierced in the wall into which men insert their penis, so that it can be satisfied by an unseen hand or other organ on the other side. A marvelous invention that preserves anonymity while at the same time increasing the pleasure of the act by preventing one from knowing who is relieving him, whom he is serving. An equivalence of hands, orifices, penises.

The attraction of swingers' clubs is that they make possible an overt lust in the half-darkness (like the "back room" that develops an erotics of the shadows). These places do not always escape the ridiculous, labored depravity, or the greediness without nobility of some of the participants. That should not conceal the strange beauty that sometimes emerges from these congregations of initiates who are bound together by the same will to abolish all individual barriers.

"The very first men I knew immediately made me the emissary of a network all of whose members cannot be known, the unconscious link in a family organized biblically. . . . Every time, I had to adapt to a different epidermis, a different complexion, a different hairiness, a different musculature; in every case, I was without hesitation, without ulterior motives, available by all the orifices of my body and to the whole extent of my consciousness," writes for example Catherine Millet, who dreamed, she tells us in a striking phrase, of being "a cumbag for a bunch of restless conventioneers." Thus the body of each individual belongs to all, and this fusion can reach grandiose heights when several dozen persons are palping one another, embracing, rediscovering a happy primitive confusion. The pleasure of being only a single people copulating, a great associative animal that surrounds communions of the flesh with a mutual good will.

Moreover, why not establish, on a voluntary basis, a free civil love service in which the men and women best endowed by nature would give their all for their admirers? This would have nothing to do with the saints of yesteryear, who were immersed in mortifications and scorn for the world, since it would be a matter of sanctifying basic appetites. Has chance given you an interesting face, a spectacular anatomy, a sublime bust or posterior? Pay off this debt while you're young by devoting yourself body and soul to those who ask you to. Demolish by generosity that fatality that dooms most of our fellow humans, especially if they are poor or unattractive, to be deprived of caresses and pleasure.[21] Become public beings in the best sense of the term.

Let Them Enjoy

According to Plato, Sophocles, at the age of eighty, was glad to be freed from the cruel yoke of desire, an experience analogous to that of a people that overthrows its tyrant, or of a slave who is freed by her owner. Inversely, the utopian writer Charles Fourier wrote around 1820:

> Humanity, after the season of love, merely vegetates, thinks as little as possible about the mind's wishes; women, too little distracted, feel this truth bitterly, and with the decline into old age seek in [religious] devotion some support from this god who seems to have moved away from them along with their cherished passion. Men succeed in forgetting love but do not replace it. The vanities of ambition and the sweetness of paternity are not equal in value to the truly

divine illusions that love provides in one's prime. Every man in his sixties glorifies and regrets the pleasures he experienced in his youth, and no young man would want to exchange his love affairs for old men's distractions.[22]

Today, we have teenage versions of Sophocles who abstain and adult versions of Fourier who do not renounce sexual desire. Something fundamental has changed in our relationship to time: we have gained two additional decades of life, and prolonged the charms of desirability for everyone. That means that it's never all over, that emotions resist the verdict of age. For those who missed out on it when they were young, there is always a catch-up class. At any age, doesn't true wisdom consist in falling in love again (even if it is with one's long-term companion)? What is there beyond such a pleasure, if not the hope of another, at once identical and different pleasure? Who would not be prepared to give everything to experience once again the marvelous moments of a nascent inclination?

Whether episodic or enduring, our love affairs teach us nothing: their chaotic succession does not culminate in a sentimental education. We aspire to only one thing: to relive them over and over, forever. One is not grown up when at the age of fifty he becomes infatuated with the first available person who comes along, as if he were twenty: the same petulance, the same stupefaction. If being adult means being capable of stability, then we suffer from chronic adolescence. We are consistent in our amorous transports and frivolous in our relationship to time. The essential point is not to reintroduce, as a kind of contraband, the spirit of fanaticism, and to fight for a world that delights loving souls and makes the ardent happy, in which Platonic affection and ethereal relationships find their place alongside the most vigorous physical embraces. Let anyone who wants to avoid sexual relations do so with full legitimacy, and let others have sexual relations with whomever they choose. Let them enjoy: the chaste and the passionate, the shy and the forward. Let us never lose the sense of the miracle of the flesh: Eros is the power of life that binds together what was separate, the sole universal language that we all speak, a dazzling short-circuit that throws bodies into contact with each other.

That it is possible to desire without loving or to love without desiring is self-evident; most of our relations with friends and family are not sexualized. But the adepts of the fusion of sex and sentiment seek in reality to subordinate the former to the latter in order to excuse or amend it. The real tragedy consists in eventually ceasing to love and to desire, and thus drying up the twofold spring that connects us to life. The contrary of the libido is not abstinence, it is *Lebensmüdigkeit*, being tired of living.

Don't Judge

Fleeing those who love us; loving those who flee us. Cursing the person who sleeps beside us, tearing her to shreds and waking up calmed, as if daylight had washed away the hatred. Going crazy about someone who despises us in proportion to our adoration for him. Looking on the slightest liaison from the point of view of its end, entering a love affair like a passenger on the *Titanic* who has a presentiment of disaster. Dreaming of sublime adventures, of wild love affairs, and stewing in suffocating confinement. Knowing only how to give, never receive, and being astonished by how badly our gifts are received. Marrying for security, not marrying for adventure, noticing that marriage protects us from nothing, and that not marrying does not guarantee the unexpected. Putting up with lies and deceptions for years and then, for a trifle, leaving forever. Hoping to find conjugal warmth in philandering, dreaming of torrid adventures in the calm of the family home. Loving at the expense of the other, absorbing her energy, stealing her youth from her, prospering from her decline. Promising ourselves every morning to leave the other and then holding on in this way for twenty years, always nourishing the idea of breaking up. Being made a fool of, being the schmuck everyone laughs at, being blind to the obvious, and adapting to it. Seeing marriage as hard work, forcing ourselves to love our spouses, enduring, suffering, accepting, and then suddenly giving it all up for a passing fancy. Sleeping with several persons without telling them, demanding that each of them adore us and no one else. Not being sure of anything, neither our sexual orientation nor our attachment, living in the country of "maybe," of sentimental hesitation, being only a question mark that says: "I love you." Weeping over the departure of someone whom we thought we didn't care about and who didn't care a fig for our heart. Venerating when he is dead a person whom we abused when he was alive. Expending immense amounts of amiability on perfect strangers, offering them sumptuous gifts, while being icy and stingy with those to whom we are close.

Those are a few of the inconsistencies of love. Why should we think it would be otherwise? To speak of love is always to start out from one's own internal disorder, to dig around in the muddy bottom of one's soul full of baseness and nobility. Let us examine the follies of the human heart without judging them. ■

PART IV

The Ideology of Love

CHAPTER 9
Persecution in the Name of Love: Christianity and Communism

The scoundrel uses the torch of love to ignite the
torch of vengeance.

MARQUIS DE SADE, *Les Crimes de l'amour*

Consider the faces of the great Christians: they are
the faces of great haters.

FRIEDRICH NIETZSCHE

In the sixteenth century, in Saragossa, Spain, a rabbi is lan-
guishing in a dungeon where he has been tortured by the
Holy Office to make him deny his faith. A Dominican friar,
the third Grand Inquisitor of Spain, followed by a skilled
torturer and two assistants, comes in tears to announce
that his "brotherly correction is over": the next day he is to
be burned at the stake along with forty other heretics, and
he must commend his soul to God. Shortly after this visit,
the prisoner notices that the door of his cell is not locked;
hardly daring to believe it, he hesitantly opens the door and
sees a long, corridor dimly lit by torches. He creeps along
it, dreading discovery. After long minutes of crawling, he
feels a draft of air on his hands and sees before him a small

door. He stands up and pushes on it. The door opens easily and gives onto a garden perfumed by lemon trees. It
is a magnificent night, the sky is studded with stars. The
rabbi, exhausted, but his heart swelling with hope, thinks
he has been saved. He already imagines himself escaping
into the nearby mountains, breathing with delight the air
of freedom. Suddenly, two arms surge up out of the darkness and seize him; he finds himself clasped to the breast
of the Grand Inquisitor. The latter, weeping and speaking
as though he were a good shepherd who has found a lost
sheep, whispers in the rabbi's ear, with a breath spoiled by
fasting, "Well, my child, so you wanted to leave us on the
day before your possible salvation?"[1]

This extraordinary story by Villiers de l'Isle-Adam tells
us something essential: long before communism and its
Moscow trials, Christianity, in its Roman Catholic version
at least, had invented persecution in the name of love.

The Church Martyred, the Martyrizing Church

The genius of Christianity was not only to give life meaning, as every religion does, but also to say to everyone: you
are not alone, God is there for you, he watches over and
protects you. "Even the hairs of your head are all num-
bered" (Matthew 10:30), Jesus says in the Gospels. Thanks
to the work of historians (Michel Foucault, Peter Brown),
we know that Christianity did not invent puritanism, but
instead borrowed it from Antiquity, just as it borrowed its
distrust of passion. But to this rigorism it adds an essential dimension: the God of love who can be "sensed by the

heart" (Pascal), and who speaks with each of his creatures in particular. But it immediately distinguishes two kinds of love: human love, which is an illusion because it leads mortals to think they are immortal, and divine love, the sole authentic one. False love that attaches itself to the creature is sensual desire (*cupiditas*), while the love that attaches itself to the Creator is charity (*caritas*). The former takes as its object a fleeting good whose slave it becomes, the latter an eternal good that frees one from fear and from death. It is madness to love humans in their human condition, says St. Augustine, to love someone who must die as if he will not die. In his *Pensées*, Pascal returned to this idea with a touch of affectation: "Do not attach yourself to me, for I am going to die; go instead in search of God."

Once this distinction has been made, an enigma remains: how could the Church, whose message is adoration, have gone astray in the Crusades, engaged in mass murder and the Inquisition? In general, these deviations are explained by history: an earthly institution connected with the established powers, Rome is supposed to have betrayed the teaching of the Gospels, recognizing its error only belatedly, at the Vatican II Council (1962–1965). In his *Brothers Karamazov*, Dostoyevsky imagined a Jesus who has returned to Earth and been arrested by the Grand Inquisitor for inciting people to seek the truth. Here, I propose a different thesis: the Church did not betray the Gospels, it fulfilled them. The worm was already in the apple in the New Testament's thoughtless praise of love as an absolute marvel. Let us recall the facts: Hardly had the Church ceased to be persecuted, thanks to Emperor Constantine I, whose Edict of Milan (313) proclaimed religious tolerance for

Christians, when it began to persecute in turn, first the pagans, then the Jews—those false friends, Augustine called them—and, over time, every group that opposed it, beginning with Christians who adhered to other sects. These acts of violence, in the form of wars and pogroms, did not really stop until after the French Revolution, once Rome and the other churches had been dispossessed of their temporal prerogatives. To put the point crudely, when Theodosius's edict of 380 made Nicean Christianity the state religion, it was love that took power. Love in the strict sense of the term: not its mask or simulacrum, but love itself, sublime and abominable at once.

Victims becoming torturers is such a classic historical pattern that we could formulate, regarding any revolution whatever, this iron law: combat oppression; beware of the oppressed. People talk about the primitive Church of the catacombs, whose existence contradicts the image of an opulent, dominating Church after Constantine. But the former contains in germ the excesses of the latter: in fraternity lie the seeds of despotism. As soon as St. Paul decreed, in a famous phrase, that in the Christian world, "There is neither Jew nor Greek, there is neither slave nor free, there is neither male nor female" (Galatians 3:28), he extends the mantle of love potentially to all: no one will escape this implacable pastoral care. It mattered little that Tertullian wrote in 212, "it is foreign to religion to coerce to religion," or that Constantine declared, according to his biographer Eusebius, "Let no Christian take his private conviction as a pretext for tormenting his neighbor"; attention was paid to neither of them.[2] Rome had erected to a position of command a sentiment that encouraged intransigence. Killing out of love was the crime of Christianity as a whole: that explains the atmosphere of great moral gentleness with which these crimes were perpetrated, the unctuous tone of the torturers, who, like the twentieth-century political commissars of real socialism, sought not merely to punish but to edify, straighten out, and amend the unbeliever. If all men are my brothers in God, I have an obligation to bring them into this family from which they have wrongly turned away, I must coerce them for their own good. This is the famous "compel them to come in" (Luke 14:16–24) that compares the kingdom of God to a wedding celebration to which certain guests decline the invitation.

A Debt That Cannot Be Repaid

Here we find a twofold movement. On the one hand, Christianity shapes the landscape of love in the West, the passionate relation between the believer and God. An admirable legacy: the sentimental word proceeds from the Judaism of the Bible (*The Song of Solomon*), the vocabulary of gallantry is modeled on that of religious devotion, and the ardor of the great female saints, the brides of Christ, foreshadows the most passionate poems in our literature. A great tradition of ravishment and ecstasy that we find in the poetry of the troubadours, in quietism, in Romanticism, and in surrealism, and which elevates love to the rank of the sacred, transforms a fleeting sentiment into an eternity of piety. "Every wealth that is not my God is a dearth to me," said St. Augustine, for example, exhorting us to adore the One who loved us even before we were born and who sent his only-begotten son to save us from our sins. The existence of God is in itself both a favor and a fervor. God is a kind father, a capricious lover whose obscurity will we have to decipher, but also a jealous tyrant who asks us to break all ties in order to follow him. "If you understand, it is not God," said Augustine,[3] an extraordinary sentence that the former chairman of the U.S. Federal Reserve, Alan Greenspan, echoed when he told the press, regarding an economic crisis: "If you understood what I said, then I must have misspoken." In short, this "hidden god" (Pascal) whose ways are impenetrable reminds us very much of the strategy of the coquette who leads her suitors by the nose and entices them the better to dismiss them. Deciphering God's will, even when he remains silent, becomes his servants' risky study; if he remains silent, that is another way of speaking, and if he speaks, it is in an obscure language that one must avoid taking literally (Simone Weil).

But this God died for our sins through the figure of the Messiah. Christ was crucified for each of us in particular. "I thought of you in my agony," Pascal has Jesus say, "I shed these drops of blood for you."[4] On the pious images that children are made to kiss in the catechism, we find the iconography of the glowing red Heart of Jesus.[5] We all have the Savior's blood on our hands, and we have contracted a debt to him that cannot be repaid, as Nietzsche saw. How can we bear such a burden of debt that weighs upon us as soon as we are born, and resembles a kind of endless blackmail? "God, whom no one will ever repay what he, without owing anything, paid for us," Augustine wrote. It is a gift with no possible counterpart: to be born is to appear before the Creator as heir to the sinful legacy of Adam. The

human race is in the situation of a slave who can never sufficiently thank the person who allowed him to be freed, and
has passed from an involuntary dependency to a voluntary
gratitude. Thus we are the Lord's hostages forever: he made
himself wretched and ignominious to save us, and we cannot refuse him our affection.

Fraternity or Death

Christ's sacrifice thus makes intolerable the half-heartedness
of believers and the error of unbelievers: once the Revelation
has taken place, how could people not want to be saved,
if necessary against their will? Such is the violence of the
divine gift, which turns out to be crushing. Eager to carry
the Good News to the whole world, Christianity, born in
the blood of martyrs, grew in the blood of others, including
that of its schismatic brothers, whether Orthodox, Cathar,
or Protestant, and thus inaugurated the aggressiveness of
Western culture. Especially since Rome, the seat of the
true religion, is in Latin *Roma*, a palindrome of *amor*, love.
Didn't Pascal himself compare the order of charity to the
destructive sword used by Jesus to overthrow human societies? Pagans have to be forced to believe, St. Augustine said:
by pretending to believe, they will end up becoming actual
believers.[6] And in *Contra Faustum*, he justifies the use of
coercion against heretics at the time of the Manichaeans
by explaining that they have to be made happy despite
themselves by bringing them back to the path of God. The
punishment of the impious has to exclude compassion. In
a letter written to the military prefect Bonifacius, who was

assigned to repress the Donatists, another heretical sect, Augustine wrote these words, which served the Church as doctrine for centuries:

> There is an unjust persecution, the one that the impious inflict on the Church of Christ, and a just persecution, the one the Church of Christ inflicts on the impious. . . . The Church persecutes out of love, and the impious out of cruelty. . . . The Church persecutes its enemies and pursues them until it has reached them and destroyed them in their pride and vanity in order to make them enjoy the benefit of truth. . . . The Church, in its charity, labors to deliver them from perdition in order to preserve them from death.[7]

Since all men are eligible for redemption, leaving them outside would be a sin, and so human souls have to be unified in a single family. It is better to coerce one's neighbor, or even to kill her, than leave her in a state of mortal sin. "Outside the Church there is no salvation," decreed the Council of Trent a millennium later, in 1545, at the time of the Counter-Reformation. Augustine provided another terrible and revealing formula: "Abstain from loving in this life in order not to lose eternal life. . . . If you have loved inappropriately, then you have hated; if you have hated knowingly, then you have loved." Hating knowingly: how can we fail to recognize in this expression, even if it was not Augustine's intention at the time that he wrote it, a call to eliminate all those who do not adhere to the true religion? Don't repeat the past, transform human relations as a whole: that is the Christian message since St. Paul, and it explains this religion's ferocity.[8] It is Christianity that has given our eroticism its warlike tone, even when our eroticism has opposed it: its belligerent pathos is directly inspired by this doctrine, and Sade is never anything but the unruly child of feudalism and a bastardized Catholicism.

Even the love that God has for his creatures is ambiguous: "Man loved by God," says Father Anders Nygren, "has no value in himself; what gives him value is the fact that God loves him."[9] A strange infatuation that begins by declaring the object of its interest null and void. It is God who is love, and not man, the fallen creature, who is lovable. He "brought you into the world," St. Francis de Sales explained in the seventeenth century, "not for any need he had of you, who are useless to him, but only in order to exercise his goodness in you, giving you his grace and his glory."[10] This makes man a being that must be corrected and amended if he remains deaf to the divine message. Killing in the name of God cannot be a crime, since God is love: anyone who remains outside his grasp is detestable and deserves punishment.

That is why medieval inquisitors, moved "by a feeling of mercy" with regard to the accused, were convinced that they were working for the latter's salvation by subjecting her to torture.[11] The same reasons that made Christianity popular—piety, collective fervor, and the hope of a supernatural destiny—made it dangerous. Hatred was able to ripple in the midst of this ocean of unlimited love that delivered disarmed victims to it. The unctuous language of prelates who had the secular authorities carry out the punishment was put in the service of a not very charitable will to power. Christianity may have invented crime based on altruism, which develops in a climate of great spiritual elevation. At least Islam is more straightforward in its certainty that it is the sole authentic belief and makes no attempt to seem to like infidels.[12] Thus we can better understand the admirable and absurd evangelical precept: "Love your enemies, and pray for those who persecute you" (Matthew 5: 44). Loving one's enemies might be taken to mean convincing one's tormentors that they are wrong;[13] but it might also be taken to mean rendering them a spiritual service by taking their lives, eliminating them out of affection for their own salvation. Pre–Vatican II Christianity or oppression in the name of love: sentimental violence, unctuous cruelty, belligerent love. We might say about it what people said in Italy about the center-right politician Romano Prodi: that it exudes benevolence through all its claws.[14]

The Community of Comrades

The notion that we are all brothers in God is an important achievement of monotheism because it established a formal equality among human beings. However, the limits of this universalism are marked out by the insistence that this fraternity must be expressed in the form of an obligatory enlistment under the same banner. Communion becomes another name for enslavement. There are many situations in which separating people is preferable to bringing them together, in which their fundamental resemblance must not conceal their desire to live separately.[15] We see to what Christianity may be compared: communism, which is its modern heresy, and which allows us to see, magnified, Christianity's defects. Marxist powers ferociously

persecuted Christians of all denominations, but they also
borrowed their principal concepts from Christianity: they
made the proletariat the worldwide Christ, the redemp-
tive class par excellence that, being nothing, must become
everything. They imagined a future society as the terres-
trial fulfillment of the promises made by the Gospels. Rosa
Luxemburg herself appealed to the Fathers of the Church,
and saw in communism the secular religion of the disadvantaged. Let us add that the two systems demand a complete
adherence that allows consciousness no area for criticism;
they practice constant quotation of the Holy Scriptures, reference to the Great Predecessors, the conflict between the
spirit and the letter, and mistrust of everything that deviates
from orthodoxy. In both cases, this world is judged in the
name of another of which people are unaware: eternal life
on the one hand, the classless society on the other. On that
basis, those who resist can be imprisoned or killed in the
name of a future happiness that they do not know but with
which they have to be inculcated. Harmony achieved by an
iron grip: that is what these systems tell us about.

We have only recently left behind these bloody regimes
that wanted to make brotherhood among peoples the bond
par excellence, and to that end terrorized millions of people.
To bring human beings together, we have to begin by excluding some of them: the miscreants, the schismatics, the
exploiters. In both cases, we find the same criminal kindness
on the part of the depositories of truth: the inquisitor, the
crusader, the political commissar. Brotherhood or death:
we know how successful this formula was at the time of the
French Revolution. People begin by invoking the Gospels—
"the first disciples of the Savior were all brothers as well,

equal and free," said the (well-named!) Abbé Lamourette in 1791—and end up sending each other to the scaffold for treason.[16] Communism, in the form of the Soviet, Maoist, Castro, and Pol Pot regimes, has practiced the elimination of comrades and fellow travelers who even on the scaffold swore allegiance to the Revolution and to Socialism. What can we do if the exquisite ideal of faith in Jesus or Lenin requires the liquidation of corrupting elements that are preventing the advent of Paradise? "O you who are my brothers because I have an enemy," said Paul Eluard, the great French Stalinist poet. Scratch the surface of discourses that laud brotherhood, analyze their tremolos: they are full of bile, of hatred; they do not cherish, they feel revulsion. It is not surprising that the last communist intellectuals in Europe, Alain Badiou and Slavoj Žižek among others, all appeal to St. Paul, to Christianity, and to the transfiguring power of love.

The ravages wrought by a rhetoric of good intentions: the misfortune of a few people matters little if it makes possible the advent of the celestial City or the Revolution. We are not guilty as soon as we are trying to do good. In Pascal's *Provincial Letters*, a Jesuit seeks to justify misdeeds by the beauty of the end sought: "When we cannot prevent the action, we at least purify the intention; and thus we correct the vicious nature of the means by the purity of the goal."[17] We can never overemphasize the number of crimes that the love of humanity in general can inspire when it is not counterbalanced by the love of human beings in particular. Self-righteous hostility that is certain that it is working for the salvation of souls or the emancipation of the oppressed binds together those it inhabits into a single ardent and implacable sheaf. This Christian God who "loves the gentle and the merciful" began by sowing behind him a terrible carnage. It is a superior attachment that justifies torturing traitors or, for communism, the elimination of enemies of the people. In modernity, there were two great systems of tyranny: by hatred, as in National Socialism, and by love, as in Marxism-Leninism, which was more difficult to refute because of the nobility of its ideals. The whole program of Nazism consisted in aversion to the Jews (and "inferior races") destined for extermination. Communism's program consisted in the emancipation of the human race via the proletariat. National Socialism spoke the language of the executioner, of the "superior race," while communism spoke the language of the victim, of the humiliated. But to realize justice on Earth, it was necessary to start by getting rid of the categories of people who opposed its advent: the bourgeois, the kulaks, the class-traitors, the imperialists, etc. The magnitude of the enterprise, carried out in the name of suffering humanity, justified the brutality of the methods. Communism was the extreme truth of a certain kind of Christianity.

The Renunciation of Proselytism

The comparison stops there, of course. Bolshevism, like its brother-enemy Nazism, raised murder to the rank of an industrial art and killed more people in one century than the churches killed in several.[18] Finally, religion is flourishing, whereas the countries in which real socialism was practiced have collapsed. What is the reason for this difference? Religion, contrary to secular doctrines, is not subject to the constraints of verification: its hopes concern the beyond, not the here and now. Christianity has been humanized in Europe, not by good will within it, but because the Renaissance, the Reformation, the Enlightenment, and the French Revolution both weakened it as a temporal power and saved it as a spiritual power. Rome has been able to courageously make its *mea culpa* by undertaking, via the Vatican II Council, a vast reexamination of its doctrine, eliminating its aggressive aspects and recognizing its most terrible errors. It took almost two millennia for the various churches of Christianity to achieve, under constraint and coercion, a certain temperance. The periods of ardent faith in the West produced not only masterpieces and incontestable advances, but also abominations and barbarity. No longing for those times of high spirituality! Christianity has become respectable again only because its fangs have been drawn (which is not yet, and may never be, the case for Islam). In its Roman Catholic, Protestant, and Orthodox forms, it has abandoned violence only because it has abandoned love as an intractable passion. The Roman Catholic Church has become, in spite of itself, a parliament obliged to arbitrate among its diverse factions. Even if it still thinks of itself as the sole depository of the true faith, it consents, not without reluctance, to criticize itself, to enter into dialogue with atheism, with agnosticism, and with other denominations. It has practiced intolerance out of passion; now it is forced to be tolerant out of weakness. Except for Islam, which remains restive, the principle of secularism is accepted throughout Europe, and for the time being there is no question of challenging it. The great religions no longer have the power, in democratic nations, to imprison or execute those who contradict them. We may find deplorable Rome's attitude regarding celibacy for priests, the ordination of women, contraception, abortion, homosexuality; we may find it irresponsible when it forbids birth control pills; and the Catholic hierarchy is positively criminal when, in the name of abstinence, it combats the condom at a time when AIDS is raging.[19]

It remains that the Church now agrees, and this is an immense progress, to dissociate love from proselytism:

> Love is freely given. It is not used to arrive at other ends. A person who practices charity in the name of the Church will never seek to impose the faith of the Church on others. He knows that love, in its purity and gratuitousness, is the best testimony to the God in whom we believe and who urges us to love.[20]

These explanations are very important: the abandonment of violent conversion is a genuine progress and explains why Christianity has become synonymous with gentleness. The more a great religion is divided, the more it gains in amiability, resigns itself to doubt and self-examination. The hope of one day seeing Christianity unified as it was in its first centuries is naïve, since the various denominations—Lutheran, Calvinist, Orthodox, and Catholic—prosper in their plurality and not in a false unity. Every monotheism someday degenerates into polytheism, the approaches to God multiply in proportion to the extent of humanity's diversification. We have to hope that the religion of the Prophet, which is already split into Sunni and Shia, will divide still further, and that the *Fitna*, discord, between its various branches, schools, and cliques will grow deeper.

We would like to be able to say of it what François Mauriac said about Germany after World War II: I like it so much that I would like to have several of them. As soon as a schism threatens a congregation—the Anglicans today, the Catholics perhaps tomorrow—we have to applaud: what the group loses in strength it will gain in wisdom, in moderation. A multiparty system is the future of the great religions. "When there is only one religion, tyranny rules; when there are two, religious war reigns; when there are many, liberty comes" (Voltaire).

What should we conclude from this episode? That more than ever, we are living under the great Christian plan, which itself was the heir of Platonism, even if we are atheists or staunchly anticlerical. To think in opposition to it is still to situate oneself in the unprecedented era that it inaugurated. Since the eighteenth century, moderns have rightly been denouncing the repression of the instincts and the misogyny propagated by the churches. But whether socialists, positivists, communists, liberals, or anarchists, they have retained from this teaching the same idea of salvation through love, entrusted with a universal mission of redemption. They have rehabilitated the flesh in the name of the same ideal of the brotherhood of hearts and the reciprocity of consciousnesses: "when the thoughts of every person will no longer have any secret for anyone" (St. Augustine). In the nineteenth century, Tolstoy, an enemy of sterile reason, argued for the regeneration of the human race by means of sentiment. At the end of the 1960s, the Beatnik poet Allen Ginsberg proclaimed that "Free love will save the world." Admitting that the world needs to be saved, it remains to find out whether affection and philanthropy will suffice.

To Have Done With . . .

THE PENIS: In 1998, Gabriel Cohn-Bendit published a pamphlet attacking the supremacy of the penis, regarded as too aggressive, and called upon his peers to abandon penetration and give priority to caressing, tickling, and sucking. The emergence of Viagra enraged this militant advocate of detumescence.[21]

THE MALE WAY OF URINATING STANDING UP: Some German feminists put up signs in toilets to force men to piss sitting down and to put an end to phallic arrogance.

THE FORMULA "I LOVE YOU": "I love you = I have you, You belong to me, You are mine," a formula of "generalized policing by love" that reproduces the traditional bourgeois family.[22]

AGAIN, THE FORMULA "I LOVE YOU": It has to be replaced, Luce Irigaray explains, by "I love *to* you" (*J'aime à toi*), a refusal of the appropriation of the other assumed by the classical declaration. "J'aime à toi" thus means "In turning around you, I take you neither as a direct object nor as an indirect object. Instead, it is around myself that I must turn in order to maintain the *à toi* thanks to the return to myself. Not with my prey—you having become mine—but with the intention of respecting my nature, my history, my intentionality, and also respecting yours."[23]

THE TWO-PIECE SWIMSUIT: In 2007, Swedish feminists demanded that they be allowed to swim topless in public swimming pools, and that this part of the female body be desexualized. From this point of view, why not propose to put bras on men's breasts or, in Muslim countries, require boys to wear veils in order to restore the balance?

HOMOSEXUALITY: The Christian Coalition, a group that is part of the American religious right, financed a newspaper advertising campaign to "cure gays." The rate of success is unknown, as is the fate reserved for those who relapsed.

THE PACS: The Pacs (Pact of civil solidarity), enacted in 1999 under the Jospin government, gave rise to right-wing demonstrations in which people brandished signs reading "Dirty Homos, Burn in Hell," "Homos to the Stake." The Pacs, according to its adversaries, will destroy the order of the family: "The right, based on the genealogical order, is giving way to a hedonist logic inherited from Nazism."[24]

LOVE AT FIRST SIGHT: "It is the whole modern conception of love that has to be reworked, as it expresses itself vulgarly but in a very transparent way in expressions like "love at first sight" (*coup de foudre*) or "honeymoon" . . . a tacky meteorology . . . colored by the most sordid revolutionary irony."[25]

ROMANTICISM: We have to stop "believing in the naturalness of love and in its romantic components, in the fixed nature of sexual roles, in possession, in exclusiveness, in jealousy, in sexual fidelity as so many proofs of love," and get beyond "the divisions of genders and sexual orientations in order to bring out new identities" and "encounter other energies."[26]

MARRIAGE, MONOGAMY: Fidelity, procreation, children, the family neurosis, prostitution, cohabitation, "quarrels, hysteria, threats, demands, violence, hatred, resentment, jealousy, rage, madness, fury, and vehemence practiced in love relationships that proceed tragically from a single negative core . . . a death drive travestied in multiple forms and always active to soil everything it touches."[27]

THE CONDOM: "Christians denounce the lie commonly called 'love.' . . . We reject the reduction of love to simian grimaces on slick paper or on the screen and to multiple and plasticized couplings, we reject the falsified loves that our time sells us. We do not want love in plastic or love under plastic."[28]

PORNOGRAPHY: "Even Hitler wasn't able to transform sex into an instrument of murder as the pornography industry has done,"[29] which is in fact an "instrument of genocide," "Dachau introduced into the bedroom and celebrated."[30]

JEALOUSY, POSSESSION, EXCLUSIVENESS: In a couple, "every sexual relationship that either partner has with a third party should be considered a joyous and pleasant experience that your partner can share in his heart and even physically."[31] ∎

CHAPTER 10

Marcel Proust's Slippers

Whatever damage the wicked do, the damage done
by respectable people is the most damaging damage.

FRIEDRICH NIETZSCHE, *Thus Spake Zarathustra*

How tiring it is to be loved, truly loved! How tiring it
is to become the burden of others' emotions! To load
with responsibilities like an errand-boy someone
who wanted to be free, always free . . . how tiring it is
to be obligated necessarily to feel something, in one
way or another, even to love a little as well, without
real reciprocity.

FRANÇOIS-AUGUSTE-RENÉ DE CHATEAUBRIAND

It is an extraordinary scene; it occurred in 1917 and has
been commented upon many times. The young Emmanuel
Berl visits Marcel Proust, whom he admires more than anyone, in order to tell him about a marvelous event. Sylvia,
the young woman he [Berl] loves, and from whom he has
not heard for four years, has replied positively to a letter in
which he asked her to marry him. The young Berl is dying
to prove to Proust that his pessimism regarding human nature is mistaken, that there are "souls in harmony."[1] But the
novelist, for whom love is only a "hallucinatory onanism,"

a self-deception in which men indulge, reacts very badly to his young friend's enthusiasm. He begins by telling Berl that it would have been better for him had Sylvia died; he would have felt a painful sorrow but it would have been less painful than the inevitable waning of her feelings. Little by little, Proust gets angry, at the risk of trampling on their friendship: he flings bitter comments at him, describes the life of "those men who have fallen to the point of living for twenty years alongside partners who deceive them without their noticing it, who hate them, who steal from them without their acknowledging it, as blind to the defects of their children as to the vices of their wives." His anger rises higher, he "throws insults at him like slippers" and orders him to leave, sends him away like someone obnoxious.

The Naïveté of Demystification

We can read this passage as a confrontation between experience and naïveté: Proust, as a mature moralist, points out that the union of souls is an illusion, while Berl still subscribes to it out of ignorance. What if it were the other way around? If Proustian blackness were only an inverted idealism? If the posture of lucidity in reality concealed a great blindness? Demystification is still part of the myth because it occupies Proust's whole work: the obstinate denunciation, page after page, of the masquerades of sentiment suggests that the case is still unsettled and that the disabused sage himself is living in an illusion. His groping perspicacity resuscitates the chimera he wants to knock down: since we are proceeding in the dark, our only grandeur consists in denouncing our lack of grandeur. It is the whole ambiguity of philosophies of suspicion that they depreciate our behaviors by postulating a perfection that is not of this world. The gigantic project of demolition undertaken by the author of *In Search of Lost Time* outlines in reverse the image of an irreproachable humanity in conformity with his declared ideals. We have to get over a final illusion, that of denouncing love as an illusion.

The same thing happens on the side of those who praise love. Read their great treatises, from Plato's *Symposium* to the homilies of St. Francis de Sales, Fénelon, and Simon Weil and on to modern writers: they are admirable but filled with dogmatism about the truth. They divide up, condemn, hierarchize, draw up gradated scales, and thus devalue what we experience. They glorify exceptional love the better to denigrate ordinary love. Whereas the moralists seek to enlighten us, the eulogists exhort us to transcend. Experts in disenchantment on the one hand, professors of the absolute on the other, they ask us to choose between everything and nothing. As they tell it, "true love" is such an ocean of marvels that alongside it there is nothing but awkward attempts, human wretchedness. The idealization of the sentiment dreamed of leads to the depreciation of the sentiment experienced. In this, we can recognize the old Christian distinction between divine *agape*, the free gift of love, without limits, and human *eros*, which is soiled with egoism and must be torn away from itself, in an ascending movement, in order to be worthy of God.[2] In the name of an inaccessible goal, we are asked to malign our awkward relationships, instead of admitting that love is nothing other than what we feel in the humble present, both precarious and magnificent.

In this domain, we have been corrupted by the mythologies of the sublime: for a long time, we have acted as if only an obstacle of a moral, political, or religious nature prevented love from flourishing in all its splendor. The obstacles have been removed and love has revealed its nature: ambivalent, admirable and pitiful. In fact, it is no more than the history of its passionate follies, as true in its wandering as in its summits. With full Romantic simpleness, Balzac, Flaubert, and Zola reveal, under the smoke screens of lyricism, a veritable Hell in which the forces of cupidity and careerism have been unleashed. But with full capitalist cynicism, Balzac also shows us a Père Goriot capable of sacrificing himself for his daughters who despise him. Flaubert shows us a Charles Bovary meeting by chance his dead wife's lover Rodolphe, and looking for some reflection of her and her warmth on his face. Zola shows us Count Muffat, inconsolable, lying on a stone bench in front of the hotel where his mistress Nana, a notorious courtesan who has taken him to the cleaners, ridiculed him, and is now dying of a horrible illness. One of the great lessons of literature: the human lack of completeness is a source of endless upheavals, and there is a descent into the lower depths of the human soul just as there is an ascent toward its grandeur, because it makes each of us capable of improving himself.

Affective Slovenliness

A generalized use of informal forms of address, the habit of calling people by their first names in business and the media,[3] the kisses widely exchanged among men in

Mediterranean countries, followed by demonstrative embraces in the manner of Mafiosi, the commercial concern of brands that offer endless promises of incessant happiness, a profusion of tears on television and radio in which everyone pecks, fondles, shakes hands, kisses, and launches into prolix, frantic confessions. We are living in a time of sentimental hysteria that throws old protocols and codes of politeness in the trashcan. It might be thought that an unprecedented wave of affection is invading our societies, even if it is to authentic friendliness what artificial aromas are to perfume. However, it would be a mistake to see this sentimentality as mere playacting, a cover for harder social relationships, or the oversensitivity of brutes. It proceeds above all from the artificial character of the relations forged in the modern city near the end of the eighteenth century, when Europe was moving into a market economy and individualism: it had to pretend to have a cohesion it lacked, whereas the bonds of clan, lineage, and corporate bodies were being undone in favor of a civility regulated by self-interest and remaining aloof.

Affectivity was established as the distance between individuals increased, breaking up the Old Regime's great sequence of alliances and reciprocities that reached from the king to the lowliest peasant. The community and the nation were no longer founded solely on blood, religious identity, or ethnic affiliation, but instead on a contract freely entered into. What was natural had to be reconstructed, social relations had to be constantly "rekindled" at the risk of collapsing. The solidarity enjoyed within the group, the village, or the family—at the price, it is true, of a lack of liberty—had now to be reaffirmed and almost acted out, at the risk of falling into complacency: nowhere is this constraint more visible than in the United States, where perfect strangers show an overflowing affection for you and then forget you just as quickly. The main thing is to display cordiality, to practice sympathy and confiding as a martial art. Smiling serves to keep others at a distance or to assassinate them under the auspices of affability. The contemporary challenge is maintaining both individual autonomy and collective cohesion without giving up either one of them.

Hence the constant urging to move beyond egoism, to reach out to others in order to make up for the defects of our condition. The result is that we are constantly taking up causes and then abandoning them, alternating between enthusiasm and indifference. But it is encouraging that communion is the ideal, whereas in earlier times, in a society based on orders and completely hemmed in by rules, the ideal of hierarchy and maintaining one's rank against the threat of indecent fusion was predominant. We are living in a time of a twofold obscenity, affective and erotic, the marriage of Bridget Jones and Rocco Siffredi, the simultaneous triumph of the cutesy and the X-rated, of chick lit and trash. A twofold irruption of sentiment and sex onto the public stage, a blast of mawkish sentimentality and hard porn, both of which *drip*, the former with tears, the latter with various liquids. But the perpetual orgy of the X-rated is no less idealistic than the drivel of saccharine romance; they both reduce the human adventure to a single dimension: that of the fluttering heart or that of complete genitality. In both cases, there is the aspiration to the sublime alongside tenderness or brutishness. Insipid paradises of the corny on the one hand and frenetic couplings on the other, both reflecting the same quest for a purity in which one would cease loving with a mixture of idealism and lust, cooing and priapism.

The Greatness of Distance

Today, love has become, along with happiness, the general ideology in the West, our Esperanto that puts everything, both sweetness and malice, under the same cloak.[4] It is the last word, all the more redoubtable because of its vagueness, the word that puts an end to discussions, the word to which there is no reply. Who, in literature, song, or film, does not praise this notion; who does not see in it the magical solution to all our problems? It is in the name of love that we punish and tyrannize, even within families, for the "good" of the child, everything is expressed in the language of intimacy, of the face-to-face, of warm closeness. The more the domain of the word *love* expands, like a sponge that is supposed to absorb differences of opinion, the more it has to arbitrate, by means of education alone, labor relations, politics, and life in the city.

But it is not love alone that binds people together, ensures the continuity of generations, and consolidates a society: it no more erases social or cultural determinisms than it replaces the institutions entrusted with putting the seal of time on ephemeral emotions. It is not love that can overcome hatred, rage, and murderous folly; instead, it is reason and democracy that channel and restrain their devastating rule. It is still less love that motivates generosity or compassion; I need not love the unfortunate person whom I help any more than I love the famished and afflicted to whom I send money or for whom I provide material support.[5] In order for something like affection among humans to manifest itself, mores, administrations, and states have to depend on a different logic that is governed not solely by the law of whims or U-turns but embodies permanence, impartiality, equanimity. It is because society is not all love and tenderness that citizens can abandon themselves to their reciprocal impulses with all the gracious inconsistency peculiar to them. The project of keeping the social order on the cutting edge of love, hoping in this way to do away with infamies and injustices, is not viable: we have to ensure that the affective order has a certain autonomy, and not confuse it with the rest.

It is love that creates our neighbor, said the eighteenth-century Swedish philosopher and theologian Swedenborg. A fine but mistaken phrase: my neighbor exists whether I love him or not, and we live among thousands of anonymous individuals who care nothing for our concern and just want to go about their business without being bothered. We do not enter into contact with most people, but only pass by them, and all their faces are not enigmas that require me to love them (Levinas) or serve them. I keep at a polite distance from them, and wish them no ill. Benevolent neutrality ought to be the *modus vivendi* of all collective life. In the city, in the family, the first imperative is assistance, but tranquility is also an imperative: don't do to others what you would not have them do to you. Everyone has a right to be left in peace. One of the great virtues of collective life is first of all what John Stuart Mill called the "no harm principle": don't meddle, don't harm, don't interfere

in others' lives. I entertain with my contemporaries all sorts
of relationships ranging from polite to passionate, including detachment and even allergy. The essential point is to
maintain the right intervals, halfway between intrusiveness
and abandonment, to erect barriers that protect individuals from their mutual expansionism. Stendhal defined society as the pleasure given to each other by people who are a
priori indifferent to one another. The great joy of public life:
interweaving with foreign universes, moving in different
contexts, delighting in passage or in transition, not being
a prisoner of any group, escaping social endogamy and the
fatalism of inbreeding. What is more stifling than groups of
people who encroach on each other and are asphyxiated by
their mutual effusions? That is no longer a society of affinities, but the swarm of the termite hill.

The Wisdom of Waiting

How can we fail to be surprised that many political officials or CEOs use the rhetoric of love and self-fulfillment
without any fear of ridicule? From Hugo Chávez exclaim-
ing "Socialism is love," to Jacques Chirac, on leaving office in March 2007, explaining in his farewell address how
much he had loved us,[6] or the Socialist candidate to succeed
him, Ségolène Royal, concluding in 2007 a rally at Paris's
Charlety Stadium with this evangelical appeal: "Let us love
each other" ("Let us love each other on top of one another"
would have been closer to the spirit of 1968), without forgetting the compassionate politics practiced by the current
president of France, who rushes to the bedside of all the

wounded, or the sermons given by the Trotskyist leader
Olivier Besancenot, who adopts Che Guevara's maxim:
"We have to become hard without ever losing our tenderness." (This is a good example of performative contradiction: the ruthless love of the revolutionary who eliminates
his enemies for the greater good of humanity.) A people
is not governed, it is cajoled, soothed, a fusional relationship of intimacy, of seduction modeled on the relationship
between parents and children, is maintained with it. Even
business enterprises adopt the same tactics when instead
of presenting themselves for what they are—profit-making
mechanisms—they claim to be radiant cities, "places where
meaning is constructed," and set out to conquer the im-
material territories of the soul, to substitute themselves for
political parties, schools, and the great forms of spirituality.
The moralizing pomposities of some big bosses reflect an
unbridled gluttony, not in financial terms but in symbolic
terms; they consider themselves the new legislators, inter-
preters of the general consciousness, producers of axioms.
Every time a government, regime, or leader yields to sentimental drunkenness, we should be wary: they're up to
something.

We've seen that the two great "civilizations of love"
(Benedict XVI) that we have known in the course of history, Christianity until the eighteenth century and communism, have not proven convincing. The twentieth century,
in its Bolshevist version, was the century of armed altruism
eager to make the human race happy in spite of itself and
falling into the spiral of mass murder. But Western democracies are guilty of the same when they yield to the universal of conversion in the name of the right to intervene. We

postulate that our values are valid worldwide, despite the fact that many countries—and not the least important ones: China, Russia, Saudi Arabia, etc.—persist in not accepting them. To the excessive indifference so visible with regard to Bosnia or Rwanda corresponds the excessive interference in Somalia in 1993 and in Iraq in 2003, when we claimed to be saving a people from famine or from dictatorship in spite of itself. Let us limit ourselves to fighting those who attack us, not compromising our principles, aiding those who explicitly request our help (as the Iranian opposition is doing today), and promoting the extension of certain rights elsewhere. But trying to deliver democracy by forceps everywhere on the globe, imposing it at bayonet point only makes people bristle. The same intoxication with the Good imbues some nongovernmental organizations (NGOs). Presenting themselves as loving hearts come to help suffering hearts, they are sometimes full of an incendiary passion that can kill those whom they claim to aid: consider for example the excesses committed in Darfur in 2007 by the French Arche de Zoé group, which tried to smuggle 103 children out of Chad to France to save them from the Sudanese tragedy, whereas they were neither orphans nor in danger.

Those who hope to see the local version of the British Parliament set up in Kabul, Beijing, or Riyadh will have to be patient and learn to acknowledge necessity. The fact that many nations still live under the yoke of arbitrary rule may dismay us; but we have to recognize the nonconcordance of time in different parts of humanity. Freedom is not a crusade; it is a proposal. If millions of people decline the invitation, that is because it does not suit them, and has to be formulated differently. It is better to persuade by example than to indoctrinate by force. Between confrontation and peace, there is a gray zone called political intelligence, which rejects both breast-beating and renunciations. In the end, as we have known since the Enlightenment, the only war that really counts is the war of ideas, which is waged day and night, in a peaceful way, undoing iniquities and breaking up hierarchies. It is that war alone, and not torture or bombardments, that modifies in depth people's ways of thinking, improves the condition of women and children, leads believers to practice their faith tolerantly and to revise the most aggressive postulates of their sacred books. But this war has a defect: it is long, and exceeds the term of a legislature; it extends over generations and even centuries. To win it through education, books, and debates, one has to use the weapons of reason and eloquence. One has to combine impatience for freedom with the wisdom to wait.

The Temptation to Be Good Is Terrible (Bertolt Brecht)

Thus we have to restrain love's impatience, its propensity to conquer new supporters. There comes a time when it has to recognize its limits, to admit that it cannot solve all problems in the realm of politics. It performs miracles, no doubt, but it has never performed the miracle of reconciling humanity with itself. It may even lead to damage worse than the vices it claims to remedy. The genius of religions will always be that they postpone until the other world the consolations that they promise here and now, for example, that "love is stronger than death": those who might confirm the truth of this claim are no longer there to do so, and they will not come back down from the Empyrean in order to reassure us. Intoxication, ecstasy, and happiness do not found a city by themselves, even if they can remotivate it. What attaches people to one another is a feeling of belonging, a community of values, a shared culture, perils overcome together, the same concern for the weak. A world united in accord with the logic of reciprocal love alone is one of those utopias that it is good to cultivate but which it would be dangerous to apply by leaping over tensions and inequalities. We have to count on a "universal sympathy" (Fourier) while at the same time being aware that it remains an unattainable horizon.

"Humanity went mad because it lacked love," Simone Weil said. There is not enough love on Earth, added the Christian philosopher Max Scheler: thus it is all a matter of quantity, of amplitude. Our poor humanity needs a massive injection of sentiments, as liquidities are injected into a bank to make it better. But there will always be enough love for people to kill each other in the name of the affection that they should have for each other. The contrary of this slimy emphasis on intimacy is modesty, discretion, the ability to withdraw from the world, to secede, to not join one's contemporaries in effusions that are as ephemeral as they are demonstrative. Let us repeat: it is better to separate individuals than to bring them together by force into a single bloc united by aversion to a third party. We now have to learn that cruelty can have many components, including the most generous ones, and that the fanaticism of the idyll is just as dangerous as that of scorn. We must not let one virtue, even if it is admirable, dominate the human family, for fear that it turn into its contrary. The ideology of love, a metaphor for all the uncertain affiliations of the democratic age, cannot become a substitute for political ideology, which itself emerged from the age of theology. We have to have done with love as a religion of earthly salvation, the better to celebrate it as a mystery of private happiness. Let us reserve the use of this term for our intimate relationships: the love of the nation, of the people, of the exploited, of humanity—all these loves, for all their pompous majesty are too vague not to be susceptible to abuse. Once this separation of orders is accepted, everyone is free to abandon himself to the plenitude of hearts, to the disordered power of attractions.

The Body, a Baroque Ornament

The body, in the name of which young people revolted in the 1960s, has been less liberated than standardized, subjected to regular exactions. Now it is, beginning with infancy, the object of ruthless surveillance; it is celebrated in appearance the better to take revenge on it, to prune it like a French garden. Consider the tendency of European women and some gay men to remove all their body hair: a meticulous attack on hair, which, whether in the armpits or elsewhere, is pulled out like a vestige of the Middle Ages, a dream of once again having skin like a baby's. We note that the same society that advises bestiality in bed also tracks down the slightest trace of hair, of animality on the skin, criminalizes odors, and wants us to be polished, scoured, and almost sterilized. Woe to anyone who still dares to display a little tuft in his or her armpit. Manes soaked with sweat, odorous refuges for delicate noses, all that is supposed to disappear in the name of decency and hygiene.

The body in its tragic and magical dimension, with its secretions, fluids, and corruption, is found today in a certain French women's literature (Catherine Cusset, Claire Legendre, Lorette Nobécourt, Claire Castillon, Nina Bouraoui). This is my soul, classical writers have said since Montaigne. This is my sex, say these contemporary adepts of auto-fiction, as if female sexuality were first of all an enigma for women themselves. For example, let us consider the taboo on full-figured women, while fashion promotes flat-chested beanpoles to the status of queenly splendors. The triumph of the emaciated mannequin, a pure vertical, the icon of a dream of disincarnation that runs through our time. This flight from matter leads to a simultaneous explosion of anorexia and obesity. The body takes revenge on its correctors by extinction or by fatty proliferation, it shrinks or it dilates. The strange thing about the anorexic is that by trying to escape physical necessities, she makes her skeleton visible. Her slender, fragile limbs remind us of a cadaver. She wanted to be an angel, a pure spirit, and she ends up a living dead person, a pile of sharp bones.

So that being curvy, that intermediate stage between being obese and being skinny, seems the most desirable state of the body, a kind of luxury of flesh that surges up, profuse and wanton, sprouting in all directions. Whereas excessive weight blurs forms and desexualizes people, curves emphasize forms, encase them. The softness of a cheek, which reminds us of childhood, the swell of a belly, the taper of a plump thigh, the pronounced roundness of a derriere all invite caresses and touching. A harmonious distribution of volumes and masses combines grace and generosity: consider, for example, the American cartoonist Robert Crumb's robust women, hefty coeds with big ankles. True beauty does not lie in conformity to canons but in the vertiginous diversity of physiognomies. Desire likes the superfluous, the plump, and it likes still more the strangeness of certain organs that enchant us in proportion to their excess: phenomenal rumps, enormous breasts, disproportionate genitals. The body then enters into the dimension of the fabulous. It may deviate into soft hugeness or obesity, or into the redundant, as in bodybuilding, which with its protuberant tendons reminds us of the classical imagery of the flayed ox (a hypermuscular athlete is a being without a skin, like a glove turned inside out), or again into the short-circuit, as in the case of transsexuals, macho men with vulvas, women with penises, Hercules with huge breasts. Where do we see the body? Neither in magazines nor in fashion shows but in the street, on the beaches. The summer is the season par excellence for unveiling treasures beneath the thin fabric of skirts and T-shirts. We allow ourselves to be caught up by these fascinating protuberances, these baroque ornaments that elude the criteria of the beautiful and the ugly, of the regular and the aberrant.

In love, an abundance of goods is not disadvantageous. ∎

EPILOGUE

Don't Be Ashamed!

The same obsession haunts the liberators of desire and the defenders of good morals: that of curing. For the former, the feeling of its taboos; for the latter, the society of hedonism. But our passions continue to rebel against the progressive vulgate that admonishes and against the backward-looking vulgate that castigates; they unfurl, heedless of whether they are moral or in conformity with the movement of history. The conquests made by feminism will not be reversed, but neither will we move beyond love at first sight, the couple, fidelity. Love is not sick, it is exactly what it should be, at every moment, with its abysses and its splendors. It is still that part of life that we do not control, that continues to resist indoctrination and ideologies. We will not save it from the wounds that affect it, the exclusions that it practices: it remains impure. Eliminate the ambiguity and you kill the enchantment. We have to keep what is best in it, its vitality, its power to weave connections, its Dionysian affirmation of life, which is simultaneously exquisite and painful. And we have to find in the interminable nonresolution of its problems the charm of a possible solution. The wisdom of love, the sacredness of the heart, the transcendence of the private sphere—the temptation is great to bring this sentiment into the realm of reason, feeling, or ethics, as was done in the eighteenth century. But there is no need to weave so many laurel wreaths for it: it can take care of itself. There is progress in the condition of men and women, there is perfectibility of the individual, there is no progress in love. It will always be a surprise. That is the Good News of the current century.

When we arrive at the evening of our lives, we suspect that we have sometimes acted badly. We did not say the right things to a friend who needed to hear them, to the child who was entrusted to us; we have abandoned people in distress, wounded those who were dear to us. We have been, by turns, cowardly and mean, but also sometimes noble and generous. Such is the abundance of the heart that amid so much pettiness it is still capable of making us better, of raising us above ourselves. To all those who are racked by the fear of deception of mockery, we must repeat: don't be ashamed of your contradictions or of being who you are, naïve, ingenuous, faithful or inconstant. Don't allow yourself to be intimidated! There is more than one road to joy.

We love as much as human beings can love, that is, imperfectly.

Pascal Bruckner's Paradoxes

The Paradox of Love constitutes the central and most ambitious of three recent works by Pascal Bruckner devoted to the subject of love in its many and varied manifestations in contemporary European and Western culture. The other two works are a short novel published in 2007 titled *Mon petit mari* (*My Little Husband*), a contemporary fable dealing with the pitfalls of marriage and parenthood, and a brief essay published in 2010, *Le mariage d'amour a-t-il échoué?* (*Has the Marriage of Love Failed?*).

In writing about love, Bruckner is of course taking on a vast subject that has been exhaustively discussed and analyzed by writers from all over the world for millennia. In France and in francophone literary culture more generally, Bruckner is following in a long tradition that includes the greatest philosophers, novelists, and *moralistes*, from La Rochefoucauld, Madame de Lafayette, and Jean-Jacques Rousseau to Stendhal and Flaubert and, more recently, Denis de Rougemont, René Girard, Tzvetan Todorov, and Alain Badiou, among others. Readers of *The Paradox of Love* will easily recognize the influence of Denis de Rougemont in particular, whose *Love in the Western World* remains one of the greatest treatises on love ever written. They will also recognize the influence of René Girard, whose concepts of mimetic desire and scapegoating have helped shape

Bruckner's perspectives not only on romantic love and desire but on a number of other topics as well.*

What distinguishes Bruckner's meditations on love, certainly in comparison with other recent French efforts along these lines, is first the scope, range, and application of his approach. As *The Paradox of Love* amply demonstrates, that approach is at once philosophical, psychological, sociological, historical, political, and literary. The essay fairly bristles with references to philosophical works by Rousseau, Spinoza, Nietzsche, and Fourrier, among many others. It relies as well on data provided in sociological surveys, observations culled from novels by novelists from France and abroad, reflections on an array of ideological and political treatises and practices, and finally, an examination of the historical impact of Christianity and the Catholic Church on European attitudes toward love and marriage.

It is perhaps in relation to the topics of religious and political practices and beliefs—and to those of Christianity and Communism in particular—that the second distinguishing feature of Bruckner's critical approach becomes most evident. This is his fascination with, and rigorous exploration of the contradictory, the paradoxical, in the subjects he analyzes. Exposing and exploring contradictions and paradoxes is, in fact, at the heart of Bruckner's critical method. Where Christianity and communism are concerned, their centrality is evident in the title of the first chapter of part IV of *The Paradox of Love*: "Persecution in the Name of

---

*See, for example, Bruckner's analysis of the West's surprising malaise in the wake of the collapse of communism and the Soviet Union in particular in *Melancolie démocratique*. For Bruckner, the source of the problem is that the West lost a global rival that pushed it forward as well as a convenient scapegoat on whom all the world's ills could be blamed.

Love: Christianity and Communism." On the topic of Christianity, Bruckner argues provocatively that while Christian faith preaches love and a generous inclusiveness, it has all too often encouraged hatred and exclusion. In this regard, Bruckner cites Nietszche to the effect that the faces of "great Christians" are not those of lovers of humankind, but those of "great haters." Moreover, Christianity's methods are coercive rather than welcoming, even, and perhaps especially for, the faithful. Of Christ's self-sacrifice and crucifixion, Bruckner writes: "we are the Lord's hostages forever: he made himself wretched and ignominious to save us, and we cannot refuse him our affection."

Communism fares no better in Bruckner's analysis. While ostensibly a profoundly generous ideology and world movement intended in the end to better the lot of all humankind, in practice it has proven murderous beyond all imagination. Moreover, like Christianity, it has functioned historically not by including all peoples but by brutally excluding many, those labeled and condemned—scapegoated—as "miscreants, the schismatics, the exploiters." At the heart of both communism and Christianity, one finds in Bruckner's view not true goodness but the "criminal kindness" of "the inquisitor, the crusader, the political commissar."

Bruckner's "paradoxical method," so to speak, has also served him well in earlier works dealing with topics including French anti-Americanism and its psychocultural and historical roots, the hypocrisies of *tier mondisme* ("Third Worldism"), and the excesses and dangers of France's and Europe's preoccupation with the so-called duty to memory. Where French anti-Americanism is concerned, Bruckner argues that the attitude itself, certainly in its more recent manifestations, derives not from a sense of cultural and historical superiority, as one would think, but from a deep-seated Schelerian *ressentiment* and feeling of political impotence. It is ultimately a sign not of French national self-confidence and self-assurance where the nation's place in the world is concerned, but rather it reveals a paralyzing self-hatred that attempts to pass itself off as its opposite.*

Similarly, Bruckner's examination of French and European Third-Worldism in early works like *Le Sanglot de L'homme blanc* (1983) (*Tears of the White Man*, 1986) relies on a highly critical analysis of the contradictions and hypocrisies of the movement itself. Ostensibly a 1970s and 1980s ideology that championed, indeed idolized, the peoples, leaders, and politics of formerly colonized countries and emerging non-Western global powers, most notably Mao's China, *tier mondisme* attracted some of France's most legendary intellectuals, including Jean-Paul Sartre and Michel Foucault. But for Bruckner what paraded itself as a revolutionary idealism and an openness to other peoples and races outside the European context was in fact a fraud, a hoax. It provided the European *tier mondiste* with a pretext for denouncing European history and culture (and thus offered him or her another opportunity to give voice to thinly disguised self-hatred) and promoted a criminal blindness that allowed the *tier mondiste* to ignore the horrendous crimes visited by leaders of Third World countries on their own people. Pol Pot's genocide in Cambodia is a

*For a recent discussion by Bruckner of French anti-Americanism, see his "The Paradoxes of Anti-Americanism" in *South Central Review*, vol. 24, no. 2 (Summer 2007), pp. 15–25.

good example. Finally, despite its apparent humility and respect for formerly colonized peoples around the world, *tier mondisme* in Bruckner's view papered over what was in reality a superior, condescending, and ultimately indifferent attitude toward those Franz Fanon had labeled "the wretched of the earth."

Bruckner's dissection of the contradictions and hypocrisies of *tier mondisme* in the 1970s and 1980s set the stage for his more recent exploration of the excesses and abuses of "memory militancy" or the "duty to memory" in France and Europe, from the 1990s up to the present. In the recent essay *La Tyrannie de la pénitence* (2006) (*The Tyranny of Guilt*, 2010), Bruckner argues that what passes for a nobly humble desire to remember the victims of Europe's criminal past—and most specifically, of course, the victims of the Holocaust and colonialism—in Bruckner's view often expresses less a genuine contrition than a thinly disguised attempt to assert one's superiority by loudly professing one's own crimes in order to preach to others. Moreover, rather than promote tolerance and understanding among all peoples, the sacred status bestowed on the Jewish victims of the Hitlerian nightmare by the "duty to memory" has instead been perverted and inspired unhealthy rivalries, a "competition among the victims" that not only creates animosities between groups and ethnicities alive today, but in many instances distorts the actual historical record itself. Rather than illuminate the past as it was intended to do, the duty to memory has paradoxically all too often distorted it.

What of the paradoxes and contradictions of love and marriage themselves? These issues are of course explored in detail in *The Paradox of Love*, but they are also cast in sharp relief in the other two works of Bruckner's recent triptych devoted to love, the novel *Mon petit mari* and the essay *Le Mariage d'amour a-t-il échoué?*

As noted, *Mon petit mari* is a contemporary fable whose protagonist, the young Parisian doctor Léon, begins to shrink progressively in physical stature following his marriage, and with the successive births of his four children. Having shrunk to the size of a tiny doll, Léon only recovers his original size when at novel's end he frees himself from wife and family and sets out to start a new life. Told with both irony and tenderness, *Mon petit mari* affirms both the beauty and power of conjugal and paternal (parental) bonds and also the necessity of being free of them if the individual is to achieve true happiness.

Published a year after *The Paradox of Love*, a second essay titled *Le mariage d'amour a-t-il échoué?* (*Has the Marriage of Love Failed?*) also dissects love's paradoxes and contradictions, in this instance, those associated specifically with contemporary romantic love and marriage. In a chapter appropriately titled "The Pathologies of the Ideal," Bruckner deftly traces the often self-defeating conundrums associated with both. Speaking of romantic love, Bruckner writes:

> The difficulty with love comes from the fact that one can affirm nothing about it without at the same time affirming the opposite. The word love is formidable and fascinating because it signifies so many contradictions: abnegation and egotism, covetousness and sublimation, infatuation and constancy. It simultaneously encapsulates the desire to capture eternity in the moment, to marshal one's powers to resist the erosion

of time as well as forgetfulness, and also to realize the spontaneous combustion of the senses and the soul. Love is the desire for incandescence as much as it is the will to permanence, and both are equally true. (pp. 59–60; translation mine)

If romantic love is (hopelessly?) vexed by its many contradictions, marriage in today's world is equally burdened by unrealizable or conflicting expectations that often prove to be insurmountable obstacles to conjugal bliss. These impossible expectations concern one's partner or spouse as well as the institution of marriage itself:

Take a look at the current ideal: everything in one person, all or nothing. Let all of our aspirations be condensed into one person, or let that person be banished if he or she does not fulfill that mission. The madness consists in wishing to reconcile everything, the heart and eroticism, the education of one's children and social success, effervescence and the long haul. Our married couples are not dying of egotism or materialism, they are dying of a fatal heroism, of too ambitious an idea of what couples should be. (pp. 62–63; translation mine)

Why such an evident passion for, and critical and methodological reliance on exposing the paradoxical, the contradictory, in Pascal Bruckner's thought as well as in his writing? Most obviously, it allows him to challenge through the use of irony and occasionally pathos the simplistic assertions and truisms associated with what the French call *idées reçus*, accepted ideas or platitudes that circulate far too freely in contemporary culture. Comfortable bromides are not an option for those who read Bruckner seriously. At the same time, the delight in paradox, the elegant and eloquent exposure and dissection of the contradictory, the duplicitous, and the hypocritical that characterizes Bruckner's work links him directly to the long line of France's great *moralistes*, from la Rochefoucauld and Chamfort (both admired by Bruckner) to Camus, and many others. For all of these writers—and for Bruckner as well—the obligation and aspiration of the *moraliste* is to be both of one's time and place and to speak of, and for, what is timeless and universal in the human condition.

Bruckner's detractors in France and elsewhere have on occasion criticized the writer's taste for the paradoxical and his frequent use of a biting irony as evidence of a haughty cynicism and politically reactionary views. In style and in tone, Bruckner's writing is somewhat reminiscent of the tradition of right-wing polemicists from Léon Bloy and Charles Maurras to Roger Nimier and Jacques Laurent, among others. But to ascribe a reactionary outlook to Bruckner on the basis of style would be to seriously misunderstand his politics (Bruckner considers himself to be on the left) as well as his aims as a writer. His "paradoxical approach" is intended precisely to deflate the pretenses and excesses of misguided and rigid beliefs and ideologies, whether they be religious, political, or ideological. As *The Paradox of Love* demonstrates, it is also intended to expose and strip away the illusions and false expectations that undermine interpersonal relations and the institution of marriage itself. It is only when these obstacles have been overcome and cleared away that responsible and intelligent choices—both personal and political—can be made, when what Molière called *le juste milieu*—the happy middle ground—is finally possible.

Richard J. Golsan
Texas A&M University

Notes

CHAPTER 1. *Liberating the Human Heart*

1. Victor Hugo, *Choses vues, 1849–1885*, Paris: Gallimard, 1972, p. 410.
2. Ibid., p. 112.
3. The irony is that in July 1845, Victor Hugo, who had just been made a Pair de France by King Louis-Philippe, was caught in the act of adultery with Léonie Biard. The young lady was imprisoned at the command of her husband, an official painter, but Hugo escaped going to prison because of his status as a French peer. What happened next is even stranger: Adèle Hugo, the poet's legitimate wife—who was herself rather unfaithful and sought to take revenge on Juliette Drouet, her husband's old mistress—succeeded in getting Léonie Biard released, and a few months later received her in her salon.
4. Cited in Mona Ozouf, *L'Homme régénéré*, Paris: Gallimard, 1989, p. 142.
5. J. J. Rousseau, *Émile*, Paris: Flammarion, Book I, pp. 48–49. On the connections among the practice of mothers nursing their babies, which was new, and Europe, conjugal love, and concern about babies, see the remarkable study by Edward Shorter, *Naissance de la famille moderne*, Paris: Le Seuil, 1977, pp. 227–229. For Shorter, Rousseau is here only repeating ideas that had already long been in circulation.
6. In addition to Shorter's study already cited, see Philippe Ariès, *L'Enfant et la famille sous l'Ancien Régime*, Paris: Plon, 1960.
7. In Jean-Claude Bologne, *Histoire du marriage en Occident*, Paris: Hachette, 2005, pp. 392–393.
8. Wilhelm Reich, *La Révolution sexuelle*, Copenhagen: Sexpol Verlag, 1936; Paris: Plon, 1968.

9. Wilhelm Reich, *La Révolution sexuelle*, p. 302. Reich demanded a progressive and rational view of sexuality in the cinema and in literature.

10. Here I refer to Pascal Bruckner and Alain Finkielkraut, *Nouveau dictionnaire amoureux*, Paris: Seuil, 1977.

11. Roland Barthes, *Fragments d'un discours amoureux*, Paris: Seuil, 1977, pp. 207–211. In his *Roland Barthes* (Paris: Seuil, 1975), at the end of a pilgrimage in China with his Maoist comrades, Barthes had already written: "the Chinese: everyone is wondering (and I first of all): but where is their sexuality? . . . And then I imagine . . . that sexuality, as we speak it and in so far as we speak it, is a product of social oppression, of the evil history of human beings" (pp. 167–168). Then we discovered later on, after the publication in 2009 of his *Journal de Chine*, that he didn't believe a word of this and was horrified by his visit to the Middle Kingdom. To say in the same breath that an old-fashioned, syrupy magazine is more subversive than Sade and that sexuality is a product of the evil history of human beings is, for an intellectual who was supposed to be on the left, either to deceive people or to take delight in sailing against the current of his time.

12. According to statistics cited by Marcela Iacub and Patrice Maniglier, *Antimanuel d'éducation sexuelle*, Paris: Bréal, 2005, p. 12. Does this reflect a persistent feeling of inferiority or a desire to rise to a higher status, to find fathers capable of providing a decent income for the children that might be born of these marriages? But how many men would also like to marry women who are wealthier and better educated than they themselves are? Statistics tell us nothing on this point. (See Serge Koster, *Abécédaire du sexe et de l'argent*, Paris: Léo Scheer, 2009.)

13. One example among many: In 2009, a police officer in eastern France castrated his wife's lover. The husband, the father of five children, went to the home of the lover and his wife, knocked him unconscious, and then dragged him into the garage, where he mutilated him (AFP, 25 May 2009). A case of archaism? Perhaps, but the archaic is what remains and will never go away. We never leave archaism behind; we move from one archaism to another.

14. J. J. Rousseau, *Émile*, Book V, pp. 465 ff. This mania for philosophizing is very French. Rousseau cites a treatise by John Locke

that ends this way: "Since our young man is ready to get married, it is time to leave him with his mistress." Rousseau does not follow this wise advice and describes the daily life of his two heroes, and Sophie, in great detail.

15. We find the same disparity in an American commentator on Rousseauism, Allan Bloom, the author of *Love and Friendship* (New York: Simon and Schuster, 1993). For the record, Bloom, a great enemy of feminism and the permissiveness of modern morals, a proponent of lasting love, was betrayed *post mortem* by his best friend, the author Saul Bellow, in a book that praised him with subtle perfidy, *Ravelstein* (New York: Viking, 2000), the first example of a literary "outing." Bellow, a winner of the Nobel Prize for Literature, revealed that Bloom, a brilliant professor at the University of Chicago, liked to cruise boys, went in for luxury, and contracted AIDS, which killed him. Whereas Rousseau is brilliant in his contradictions, Bloom was a laborious impostor. There can be no book on love that does not have a consubstantial connection with its author: in this domain, lying, or rather lying to oneself, presenting oneself as an exemplary spouse or an unbridled libertine when one is neither one nor the other, is to profane the very essence of writing, to take one's readers for fools.

CHAPTER 2. *Seduction as a Market*

1. Thus on the Internet we find sites for those attracted to obese people or the very old, gerontophiles who express their hunger for dilapidated or faded bodies. A marvelous arrangement that makes it possible not to exclude anyone!

2. For example, Geneviève Fraisse, *Du Consentement*, Paris: Le Seuil, 2007, who recommends disobedience and rebellion against acquiescence.

3. In Brian De Palma's *The Black Dahlia* (2006), two characters who had earlier been friends brush their lips together during a dinner, then stand up and furiously pull off the tablecloth with all the dishes and the meal, rip off their clothes, and have sex on the dinner table. An erotic madness like the Hollywood version

of the primitive potlatch. Why buy expensive fine lingerie if the first good-for-nothing in rut is going to ruin it at a single stroke?

4. The equivalent of Romeo and Juliet today, in English-speaking countries, is love affairs between professors and students, which are absolutely prohibited. Many novels testify to this new climate, such as *Disgrace*, by the Nobel Prize–winning South African author J. M. Coetzee, and the novels of Philip Roth. Derek Walcott, a poet from the Antilles who won the Nobel Prize in 1992, had to withdraw his candidacy for the chair of poetry at Oxford after a campaign of anonymous letters repeating accusations of sexual harassment made against him more than twenty-five years earlier. But the woman poet who was appointed instead, Ruth Padel, had to resign in turn with apologies, because she had participated in this campaign of denigration. English-speaking universities have become the site of a new Inquisition that exercises a right to investigate the private life of its members and demands confession, repentance, and re-education. The Protestant world has readapted for its own ends some of the worst institutions of Catholicism.

5. Geneticists add another factor involved in the choice of mates: the "olfactive signature." Body odor is supposed to be connected with the human leukocyte antigen system (HLA system, a major complex in histocompatibility), an area of the genome that is essential to the immune system. The French expression "avoir quelq'un dans le nez" could be taken as referring both to an allergy and to an irresistible attraction. We cannot smell someone, but we sniff the beloved with delight, we breathe her in.

6. Honoré de Balzac, *La Cousine Bette*, Paris: Gallimard/Folio, pp. 172–173.

CHAPTER 3. *I Love You: Weakness and Capture*

1. Alain de Botton offers a delicious account of his love affair with a certain Chloé: "We live fully only if someone loves us. . . . Who am I if others don't whisper the answer to me?" (*Petite Philosophie de l'amour*, French translation, Paris: Denoël, 1994, pp. 168, 172.)

2. Emmanuel Levinas, *Totalité et infini*, Paris: Livre de Poche, 1990, p. 289.

3. Cf. Freud: "When one has clearly been one's mother's favorite child, one retains for life this conquering feeling, this assurance of success which in reality rarely fails to produce it."

4. Wilhelm P. J. Gauger, *Geschlechter, Liege und Ehe in der Aufklärung von Londoner Zeitschriften um 1700*, diss., Berlin, 1965, pp. 300 ff. (Quoted in Niklas Luhmann, French translation *Amour comme passion*, Paris: Aubier, 1990, pp. 196–197.)

5. On this sensitive subject, let us note that for a significant number of women, it is still up to men to pay, even after "liberation," while a consistent percentage of men find it degrading when a woman picks up the tab and humiliating when she earns more than they do. We can consider the first attitude incoherent and the second stupid. We see all the advantages of the old system and all the privileges of the new.

CHAPTER 4. *The Noble Challenge of Marriage for Love*

1. Guy de Maupassant, "Jadis." In *Contes et nouvelles*, Paris: Pléiade, 1974, vol. 1, pp. 181–185. I thank Luc Ferry for drawing my attention to this story.

2. Jean-Louis Flandrin, *Un temps pour embrasser. Aux origines de la morale sexuelle occidentale*. Paris: Seuil, 1983, pp. 83–85.

3. "Woman is a kind of property that one acquires by contract; she is movable property because possession amounts to title: she is, strictly speaking, only an annex to man." (Balzac, *Physiologie du marriage*, 1829.)

4. "I have concealed the greater part of it, from fear of tormenting you or lessening your esteem by a manner unbecoming to a husband," the Prince confesses on his deathbed, destroyed by the revelation made by his wife that she was in love with Monsieur de Nemours. (Marie-Madeleine de Lafayette, *The Princess of Cleves*, trans. T. S. Perry and J. D. Lyons, New York: W. W. Norton, 1994, p. 95.)

5. "It is time for love to become once again what it should never have ceased to be: the determining motive, the essential condi-

tion, of conjugal union. It alone has the privilege of discerning or creating accord between persons," wrote for example Charles Alric, a young republican deputy, in *Le Mariage et l'Amour au XIXme siècle*. Quoted in Jean-Claude Bologne, *Histoire du mariage en Occident*, Paris: Hachette, 1995, p. 356.

6. J.-C. Bologne, *Histoire du mariage en Occident*, pp. 354–355 and 358.

7. The "Pact of association and civil solidarity" (domestic partnership) comes closer to marriage because since 2005 it offers more flexibility but retains the same tax advantages. Originally conceived for homosexual couples, it is now used primarily by heterosexuals. In 2008, almost 140,000 Pacs were signed.

8. Let us recall a few steps in this process: In July 1965, the reform of marriage law emancipated wives from their husband's guardianship. The law of June 1970 deprived the father of his sole authority over his children, which he henceforth shared with the mother. Adultery was decriminalized on July 11, 1975, while the laws of July 4, 1975, and January 2, 1978, recognized the right of cohabitation and the law of 1985 recognized the equality of the spouses in the management of family property. (Source: André Rauch, *L'Identité masculine à l'ombre des femmes*, Paris: Hachette, 2004, pp. 202–206.) In 1972, the legislature declared the equality of legitimate and illegitimate children, and in 2001 the children's equal rights to inherit were guaranteed. In 2005, a government ordinance removed the words *legitimate* and *illegitimate* (*naturel*) from the civil code. In Spain, after a procedure for quick divorces was set up in 2004 over the vehement protests of the Church, the number of divorces increased by 74 percent in the year 2006 alone, and a majority of the filers were women. In France, one adult in three lives without a spouse, fewer than one child in two lives under the same roof as its father. Finally, one child in thirty is not the child of the father whose name appears on the birth certificate. But in order to keep children from being abandoned, the Council of State refuses to accept paternity tests.

9. Robert Musil, for example: "We are the last Mohicans of love," but also Denis de Rougemont, Roland Barthes, Octavio Paz, and Allan Bloom ("Being romantic today is tantamount to cultivat-

ing one's virginity in a brothel"), as well as many Christian and Marxist pamphleteers.

10. Denis de Rougemont, *L'Amour et l'Occident*, Paris: 10/18, 1995, p. 318.

11. André Breton, *L'Amour fou*, Paris: Gallimard, p. 136.

12. In a famous anthology published in 1956, Benjamin Péret, another surrealist, gave this definition of sublime love: "the most intransigent summit of monogamy, the highest degree of elevation, the limit. . . , a geometric place where the intellect, the flesh, and the heart melt into an inalterable diamond." This is a profane version of the most ardent Christian mysticism, that of Ruysbroek or Francis of Assisi. (*Anthologie de l'amour sublime*, Paris: Albin Michel, 1956, p. 9.)

13. "Acting against his own ideals is a fundamental trait of Rousseau's personality, because in him everything is paradoxical and subject to divergent interpretations." (Agnès Walch, *Histoire de l'adultère*, Paris: Perrin, 2008, p. 245.)

14. According to a book published in 1906 by an early twentieth-century gynecologist, A. Forel, the average duration of coitus in middle-class marriages was the same as that required to boil an egg, that is, three or four minutes. According to Charles-Louis Philippe, the author of *Bubu de Montparnasse*, which appeared in 1901, intercourse between a whore and her pimp lasted a good quarter of an hour, long enough to give them some real fun before they fell asleep. (Cited in Alain Corbin, *Les Filles de Noce*, Paris: Aubier, 1978, p. 289.)

15. Alain Corbin, *Les Filles de Noce*, pp. 281–282. Women's right to have orgasms, Theodore Zeldin explains, appeared in treatises on marriage around the beginning of World War I. (Quoted in Edward Shorter, *Naissance de la famille moderne*, Paris: Le Seuil, 1977, p. 303.)

16. The nascent science of sexology (the term first appeared in France in 1910) was concerned to combat female masturbation arising from frustration and generating adulterous affairs. (See Agnès Walch, *Histoire de l'adultère*, Paris: Perrin, 2008, p. 309.)

17. The French presidential couple's pretty coach, Julie Imperiali, was dismissed in 2009 for having revealed the secrets of this teaching to the press.

18. A study titled "Prédiction du divorce chez les jeunes mariés à partir des trois premières minutes d'un conflit conjugal," was published by psychologists from the state of Washington in 1999 in the journal *Family Process* (*Libération*, June 2, 2009). The reliability of these tests has been challenged.

19. "Réveiller votre désir," *Psychologie magazine*, August–July 2009. The suggested ways of doing so include eating cherries in bed, eating chocolate, sharing plans, giving priority to physical contact, formulating expectations.

20. Tennessee Williams, *The Roman Spring of Mrs. Stone*, New York: New Directions, 1993, pp. 32 and 29.

21. André Gorz, *Lettre à D. Histoire d'un amour*. Paris: Galilée, 2006.

22. Francisco de Quevedo, "Love Constant beyond Death" ("Amor constante más allá de la muerte"), a sonnet published in *El Parnaso español*, 1648.

CHAPTER 5. *Fluctuating Loyalties*

1. Jean Paulhan, *Entretiens avec Robert Mallet*, Paris: Gallimard, 2002, p. 31.

2. Until the end of the nineteenth century, cuckolds, especially in small villages, were subjected to public humiliation and taunting, led about on asses, covered with ordure, and forcibly shut up with their wives in their houses for two days while villagers banged with spoons and forks outside: by failing to properly supervise their wives, they were putting the patriarchal order in danger. (Edward Shorter, *Naissance de la famille moderne*, Paris: Le Seuil, 1977, p. 270.) On the other hand, people turned a blind eye to husbands' escapades, which did not undermine collective authority. Charles Fourier wrote a delicious *Hiérarchie du cocuage* (*Hierarchy of Cuckoldry*), in which he made fun of the middle-class marriage of his time and listed all the possible and imaginable types of cuckolds: the cuckold in the making, the martial cuckold, the jeering cuckold, the resigned cuckold, and the posthumous cuckold, whose wife gives birth ten months after his death.

3. See Agnès Walch, *Histoire de l'adultère*, Paris: Perrin, 2008, p. 353. Adultery was decriminalized in France in 1975.

4. Aldo Naouri, *Adultères*, Paris: Odile Jacob, 2004, p. 244.

5. Lionel Trilling reminded us that in Greek *authentos* has an aggressive connotation: it means "to have full power over" but also "to commit murder." (Lionel Trilling, *Sincerity and Authenticity*, Cambridge, MA: Harvard University Press, 1972, p. 131.)

6. Marie-Madeleine de Lafayette, *The Princess of Cleves*, trans. T. S. Perry and J. D. Lyons, New York: W. W. Norton, 1994, p. 95., p. 95.

7. Immanuel Kant, *Critique of Practical Reason and Other Writings in Moral Philosophy*, ed. and trans. Lewis White Beck, Chicago: University of Chicago Press, 1949, pp. 346–350.

8. Denis de Rougement, *Les Mythes de l'amour*, Paris: Albin Michel, 1996, p. 120.

9. See Lilian Mathieu, *La condition prostituée*, Paris: Textuel, 2006, which situates the debate in the French context and advocates, though with major reservations, the French model, which tolerates prostitution without authorizing it and punishes only procuring and soliciting.

10. The sordid affair in which Dominique Strauss-Kahn was involved in May 2011 and that will be judged in court when the time comes has once again revealed the cultural chasm that separates France from the United States. What shocked the French was the revelation of the wealth of the left-wing candidate for the presidency. The fact that he was living like a nabob at the same time that he was supposed to embody the hopes of millions of dispossessed scandalized the French more than his dissolute morals. America reacted in the inverse way: public figures are expected to be morally irreproachable. On both sides of the Atlantic, rape is a crime, sexual harassment is a punishable offense, and the prisons are full of perverts. But in the United States, adultery seems to be an indictable offense: there is no private life in this domain, as the Anthony Weiner and Arnold Schwarzenegger affairs showed again in the spring of 2011—in France, the latter were met with sniggers and shrugs. And let us add that in America, disapproval of licentious conduct is accompanied by a certain delectation: therein lies the whole ambiguity of this lubricious neo-Puritanism that pretends to be scandalized but delights for weeks in stories on television and in the print media

about sperm, fellatio, and sodomy. For Europeans, this ethics of transparency that makes everyone's private life the property of others is potentially totalitarian, as it was in the ex–Soviet Union or in Maoist China. Sex is what puts every American citizen under the virtual surveillance of all the rest. This is an unacceptable proposition for nations that have made the protection of individuals an inviolable dogma and defamation a crime.

From the Strauss-Kahn affair that occurred in spring 2011, we can learn three things. The first is that it revived the culture war on both sides of the Atlantic. Some of the most important American media engaged, immediately and without awaiting the conclusions of the official investigation, in a genuine lynching of Strauss-Kahn and through him of France, which was seen as guilty of general moral disorder. Inversely, the American court system, which was at first very hostile to the accused, proved to be more equitable, dropping the charges against the former head of the IMF on August 23 for lack of proof. Thus we witnessed the reappearance of that famous cliché of Westerns: the angry mob demanding that the sheriff hand over the suspect so that it can hang him.

The second point: This affair proved the persistence of taboos. In France, the taboo is money; on the other side of the Atlantic it is sexual desire. The sums spent by the accused for his defense shocked the French as much as his alleged aggression and his maniacal behavior. How could a man who was supposed to embody the values of the left live in such a way? In the United States, on the other hand, neo-Puritanism is now exercised in the name of the defense of minorities: it is to "protect" women that sex outside marriage is condemned, but it is condemned, as in the manuals used by Catholic confessors, only the better to talk about it. This episode proves to what extent the boundary between the private and the public and the presumption of innocence, which is fundamental to French law, remains a precious protection against a slide into totalitarianism. The intrusion of the collectivity into our intimate acts must be contained, except in the case of proven violence, because if it is not we fall into abuse. It will be interesting to see if this incident marks the beginning of an Americanization of French political life, which would not necessarily be good news.

Finally, the third point: The vertiginous fall of Strauss-Kahn, carried away by an irrepressible libido, seems to be an illustration of the Freudian theory of parapraxis. In a few minutes, a man destined for the highest office ruins, voluntarily or not, his career, his reputation, his name. And probably irreversibly: cleared legally, he will remain marked morally. The French, who were indulgent so long as Strauss-Kahn remained under house arrest in New York, are proving to be more severe now that he has returned to Paris. As for Nafissatou Diallo, whom the prosecutor's office has described as a compulsive liar, she is perhaps the most fascinating figure in this news item. She revealed gifts for acting and for making up stories that deserve to be exploited somewhere other than in cleaning bedrooms. We can only wish her the career she deserves, if her life is not spoiled by her lies. Because of the areas in this case that remain unclear and the passions that it arouses, this Franco-American affair, halfway between Shakespearian tragedy and light comedy, is worthy of the talent of a great director.

11. In the philosophical criticism of the Old Regime in France, the immorality of the court is seen as proof of the despotic power of the sovereign who wants to keep the people under his control. He is supposed to grant them moral license to make them forget their political servitude. See Agnès Walch, *Histoire de l'adultère*, p. 351.

12. Let us recall Adam Smith's foundational thesis: "It is not from the benevolence of the butcher, the brewer, or the baker that we expect our dinner, but from their regard to their own interest. We address ourselves, not to their humanity, but to their self-love." (*Inquiry into the Nature and Causes of the Wealth of Nations*, ed. D. Buchanan, Edinburgh, 1814, vol. 1, p. 22.)

13. Cf. Serge Chaumier: "Open marriage offers the equal status of the sexes, the abolition of double standards, the necessary egalitarian redistribution of tasks and of responsibility for children's upbringing. It rejects adultery and a double standard as dangerous for spouses. The conventions of the couple setting limits that are mutually granted makes it possible to discuss and to go against a double standard . . . the open couple sees infidelity more in the deception of a double standard stuck in hypocrisy than in an openly recognized relationship with a third

party. However, we must repeat that not all open couples will go so far as to accept all forms of relationship with a third party. Very complex restrictions may be involved, but the principle of openness is recognized . . . contracts are constantly rewritten in accord with the events the partners encounter." (*La Déliaison amoureuse*, Paris: Payot, 2004, p. 272.)

14. In Simone de Beauvoir, *La Force des choses*, Paris: Gallimard, 1963.

15. Let us recall the admirable closing lines of *La Cérémonie des Adieux*, a chronicle of Sartre's physical and intellectual decline at the end of his life, the ultimate reappropriation of the beloved man by writing: "His death separates us. My death will not reunite us. That is how it is: it is already a beautiful thing that our lives were able to be in harmony for such a long time." (S. de Beauvoir, *La Cérémonie des adieux*, Paris: Gallimard, 1981, p. 176.)

16. Choderlos de Laclos, *Les Liaisons dangereuses*, trans. Douglas Parmée, New York: Oxford University Press, 1995, p. 315.

CHAPTER 6. *The Pleasures and Servitudes of Living Together*

1. In India, in more advanced middle-class groups, arranged marriage is tempered by a kind of casting in which the young woman is presented to possible suitors, with whom she goes out for a few evenings under the supervision of a chaperone. Thus she can indicate her preference. Within limits, this can be compared with the eighteenth-century Finnish and Swedish practice of nocturnal wooing or "bundling," in which a group of young people, generally tipsy, made the rounds of young women's homes on Saturday nights, reciting couplets for them. Each young woman took a suitor into her bed, but he did not have the right to remove his clothes, even if kisses were permitted. We do not know how far this flirting went, or what intimacies the young woman allowed. Thus each woman could form an idea of the candidates for her hand before making her choice of a specific individual. A girl might have had forty or fifty boys in her bed before making up her mind. (Edward Shorter, *Naissance de la famille moderne*, Paris: Le Seuil, 1977, pp. 129–130.)

2. One consequence of women's entry into the workforce: in 1977, the average age of women giving birth was 26.5; today, one child in five is born to a mother 35 or over. In France, 1.6 million children, or one in ten, live in blended families; 2.7 million, or one in four, live in single-parent families, usually with the mother; and 30,000 live in a home with two adults of the same sex.

3. In this respect, Christianity is a dizzying family romance: Mary is the mother of Jesus, but she is also his daughter, because she is the daughter of God but also his spouse, in a double symbolic incest. Having conceived without sexual intercourse, enjoying a perpetual virginity, she offers a striking example of parthenogenesis. The son has thus created his mother, who was moreover inseminated by the Holy Spirit, thus becoming the first woman pregnant with History. On this subject, see the convincing study by Pierre-Emmanuel Dauzat, *Les Sexes du Christ*, Paris: Denoël, 2008.

4. Luc Ferry, *Familles, je vous aime*, Paris: XO Editions, 2007.

5. A few figures for France: According to statistics published by the Ministry of the Interior on June 15, 2009 (source: *Journal du Dimanche*, June 14, 2009), a homicide is committed within a couple every two days. In 2008, intrafamily violence resulted in the deaths of at least 280 persons (including children, collateral victims, and the suicide of the perpetrators) and injury to 180,000 more. Women are the most frequent victims: every sixty hours, a woman succumbs to the violence of her ex or her companion (156 in 2008), and one man is killed every fourteen days (27 in 2008). The causes are multiple: alcoholism, illness, unemployment, a rejection of separation. The departments most affected are Nord, Gironde, and Seine-Saint-Denis.

6. See Laurent Greisalmer, "Au nom des mères," *Le Monde*, May 29, 2006.

7. See Caroline Thompson's very informative analysis, *La Violence de l'amour*, Paris: Hachette, 2006.

8. I refer the reader to Alain Finkielkraut's excellent book, *La Sagesse de l'amour*, Paris: Gallimard, 1985, in which the author analyzes this notion drawn from the philosophy of Levinas while at the same time warning against his errors.

9. Allan Bloom, *The Closing of the American Mind*, New York: Simon and Schuster, 1988, p. 120.

10. Anthony Giddens, *The Transformation of Intimacy: Sexuality, Love, and Eroticism in Modern Societies*, Stanford, CA: Stanford University Press, 1992.

11. Louis Antoine de Saint-Just, *L'Esprit de la révolution*, Paris: 10/18, 1988, pp. 58–59.

CHAPTER 7. *Is There a Sexual Revolution?*

1. On the occasion of the 200th issue of *Elle*, a journalist, Jean-Pierre Elkabbach, asks a reader: "And you madame, are you a slut?"—"Alas, no," she replies.

2. These magazines offer multiple counsels for rising in society ("Do you have to sleep with someone to succeed?"; "Succeeding when you've got big breasts") for female careerists and indices of social standing. The world used to be divided between those who did it and those who didn't; now there is what it's cool to do and what isn't. The Summer 2008 issue of the monthly magazine *Marie-Claire* published an erotic guide for liberated women in which all the possibilities are listed: triolism, swinging, prostitution, sadomasochism, etc. But the official code of good manners can also lead to malice: "I hate guys who are sick," "Avoid dirty tricks," read the headlines of the magazine *20 Ans* in 1994. Sex is becoming a manual of guerilla warfare against men.

3. Sexual humiliation is not new in Europe: In Old Regime France, a husband whom his wife suspected of impotence was subjected to the test of "Congress": after being examined by a physician, he had to consummate his marriage in public while people kibitzed and matrons looked on avidly. If he failed the test, he had to pay back the woman's dowry and let her go. For the woman, it was a way of separating herself from an undesirable husband at a time when divorce was still prohibited. A castrating ceremony, the Congress was prohibited by the Church on February 18, 1677. (Jean-Philippe de Tonnac, *La Révolution a-sexuelle*, Paris: Albin Michel, 2006, pp. 92–94.) Here again, let us avoid anachronism: a husband who is impotent or has erectile problems is punished because he is not in accord with the collective order, and endangers the fecundity of the community and the institution of marriage.

4. We will not adopt here Michel Foucault's excessively reductive hypothesis that sees Western man as a "confessing animal." It is not truth that our time is looking for through its sexual obsession, but rather a certain form of immediate redemption.

5. The most recent and most complete investigation in this domain (Nathalie Bajos and Michel Bozon, eds., *L'Enquête sur la sexualité en France*, Paris: La Découverte, 2008) reveals a broadening of the repertoire of sexual acts, widespread recourse to the Internet, the abandonment of chastity before marriage, a closer correspondence between the ages of first sexual intercourse and between the number of partners for both sexes, the persistence of a male sexuality characterized by a massive recourse to masturbation, prostitution, and pornography, but also by a notable difference in practices, depending on social milieu, and the persistence of functional difficulties such as erectile problems, lack of orgasm, and anaphrodisia (pp. 485 ff.; cf. the article by Sharman Levinson in the same volume).

6. The respectable professor revealed that 50 percent of married men had had affairs, at least 37 percent had had a homosexual experience at some time in their lives, and 90 percent practiced masturbation. For women, 50 percent had had intercourse before marriage, 28 percent had carried on an extramarital affair, and 62 percent masturbated. This report caused a scandal. Dr. Kinsey, who was targeted by the American religious right at the height of the McCarthy period, died worn down by the attacks.

7. Herbert Marcuse was the first to see in "repressive desublimation" a liberation of sexuality under the sign of merchandise and business that diminishes and weakens vital erotic energy. (*Eros and Civilization*, Boston, MA: Beacon, 1955.)

8. A few examples among others: The philosopher Beatriz Preciado, who injected herself with testosterone to escape her sexual identity, claims that the difference between the two sexes is a "micro-fascism" that has to be deconstructed, and makes every woman who takes the pill "a little heterosexual whore." She violently attacks feminists and official gay movements, which she considers guilty of collusion with pharmaco-pornographic society. (Beatriz Preciado, *Testo Junkie*, Paris: Grasset, 2008.) Or again, the post-porn performance artist Annie Sprinkle,

who urges ordinary women to transform their exhibited bodies into "sites of resistance to the modern pornographic desire for knowledge." (Quoted by Marie-Hélène Bourcier, in *Dictionnaire de la Pornographie*, ed. Philippe di Falco, Paris: PUF, 2005, pp. 379–380: "By inviting male and female spectators to contemplate her cervix with the aid of a flashlight, after having introduced a speculum into her vagina at the beginning of the performance, Sprinkle reappropriates a porno-gynecological position that makes any objectivization of her body impossible.")

9. See for example the neo-feminist Wendy Delorme, *Insurrections! en territoire sexuel*, Paris: Le Diable Vauvert, 2009. Delorme is a militant advocate for whatever falls outside the norm, for the transgendered.

10. St. Augustine, *The City of God*, trans. M. Dods, New York: Random House, 1950, book XIV, p. 465.

11. Ibid., p. 473.

12. "Quand je pense à Fernande, je bande, je bande / Mais quand je pense à Lulu, là je ne bande plus. . . . "

13. See Laurent Gerbier's article on Augustine in the *Magazine Littéraire*, no. 439, February 2005, p. 60.

14. Just as the Romans proposed the lives of famous men as exemplars (*exempla*), in matters of sexuality we have a whole chronicle of more or less picaresque heroic feats: In the 1970s, the actress Sylvia Bourdon bragged that in a single day she had had intercourse with every man in an African village, a record that numerous stars of X-rated films claim to have beaten. In 2006, a masturbation session was organized in London as a protest against AIDS: participants were supposed to masturbate in public, sponsors' contributions depending on the length of time and the number of orgasms achieved. The winner was an American who retained an erection for more than eight hours, alternating between his left and his right hands. Let us also recall the porn star John Holmes, who displayed a penis 36 centimeters long, performed in more than 220 films, and racked up 14,000 female and male partners. Nicknamed "the King of Porn," he became addicted to drugs, swallowing forty Valiums a day while injecting massive amounts of cocaine into his veins. He died of AIDs

on March 13, 1988. One can hardly overemphasize the fascination with numbers and gigantic size in sexuality, which is also a matter of quantity and can always take the form of a fabulous spectacle that is presented to others. It is on the basis of these bizarre or comical fictions that the current erotic dream prospers.

15. Quoted in *Romans libertins du XVIIIme siècle*, Paris: Gallimard (Pleïade), 2000, p. XV.

16. These are a few of the infractions listed in sixth- and seventh-century penitentials. See the standard work on this subject by Jean-Pierre Flandrin, *Un temps pour embrasser*, Paris: Seuil, 1975.

17. Like the scatlogical melodrama by the German writer Charlotte Roche, *Wetlands* (New York: Grove, 2009), the story of a young woman who checks into a hospital to have a hemorrhoid operation and hopes this will permit her to reconcile her divorced parents. A baroque, coprophilic novel in which we see the heroine exchange used tampons with a girlfriend, spray herself with her strongest intimate odors, *Wetlands* constantly plays on the line between false candor and the repugnant.

18. I foresaw this movement in an article entitled "Délivrez nous du sexe" (*Le Débat* in March 1981) concerning new erotic practices, from the most benign to the most extreme. Let us recall that it was the Russian anarchist Alexandra Kollontai who compared coitus to an act as simple as drinking a glass of water. Lenin opposed her on this and many other points.

19. Sex offenders constitute more than a third of the prison population in France. The incarceration of such offenders is a factor in the overcrowding of prisons. In 1999, they represented 20 percent of those incarcerated in France; today they represent almost 30 percent. French criminal courts sometimes treat rapists more severely than murderers: the psychic murder constituted by rape is more harshly punished than physical murder because it incarnates absolute evil. (Xavier Lameyre, *La Criminalité sexuelle*, Paris: Flammarion, 2000, pp. 41, 43, 99.)

20. On the recourse to the penal as a way of moralizing society, see the important book by Antoine Garapon and Denis Salas, *La République pénalisée*, Paris: Hachette, 1996, and also Jean-Claude Guillebaud, *La Tyrannie du plaisir*, Paris: Seuil, 1998, chap. 12.

21. Sexual offenses explode as soon as a society tries to protect the person as a whole rather than the traditional, inegalitarian order with regard to women: its repressive measures implicitly assume the possibility that the two sexes have the same rights. (Xavier Lameyre, *La Criminalité sexuelle*, pp. 97–98.)

22. When during the trial it came out that the main witness for the prosecution had lied, all the defendants were acquitted.

23. "The less symbolism there is, the more legal rules there are," Michel Schneider very rightly observes in *La Confusion des sexes*, Paris: Flammarion, 1007, p. 77.

24. René Girard, *Violence and the Sacred*, trans. Patrick Gregory, Baltimore: Johns Hopkins University Press, 1977, p. 34.

25. Sigmund Freud, *La Vie sexuelle*, Paris: PUF, 1997, p. 56.

CHAPTER 8. *Toward a Bankruptcy of Eros?*

1. Like Virginie Despentes's *Baise-moi*, a cry of rage directed against the men that one kills after having enjoyed them. In Despentes, there is a kind of idealism immersed in the sordid. Robberies, rapes, random murders, beatings, and orgies are aspirations as intense as mad love and romantic passion. Despentes, or the spokesperson for the inverted sublime: in her work, savagery is like nostalgia in the fairy tale.

2. In France, 1.17 percent of women and 3.6 percent of men are said to engage in swinging, mainly between the ages of 25 and 49. (Nathalie Bajos and Michel Bozon, eds., *L'Enquête sur la sexualité en France*, Paris: La Découverte, 2008, p. 278.)

3. See the terrifying examples given in Christophe Bourseiller, *Les Forcenés du désir*, Paris: Denoël, 2000.

4. Cf. the sadomasochist contract as instituted by Sacher-Masoch and analyzed by Gilles Deleuze, *La Venus à la fourrure*, Paris: Minuit, 2004.

5. In Catholic theology, the glorious body is a spiritual body governed by the omnipotence of the spirit and endowed with four attributes: impassiveness, agility, subtlety, and clarity. These attributes are to be acquired only after the Resurrection.

6. Quoted in Peter Brown, The†Body†and†Society: Men, Women, and Sexual Renunciation in Early Christianity, New York: Columbia University Press, 1988; French trans. Le Renoncement à la chair, Paris: Gallimard, 1995, p. 422.

7. Jean-Louis Flandrin, Un temps pour embrasser, Paris: Seuil, 1975.

8. Peter Brown, Le Renoncement à la chair, pp. 55–56. For Christian groups, it was a matter of escaping the tyranny of this world and seeing that the rigid borderlines between the sexes could be dissolved in "the liquid gold of a spiritual body."

9. On this phenomenon and its scope, the standard work is Jean-Philippe de Tonnac, La Révolution a-sexuelle, Paris: Albin Michel, 2006.

10. Between 10 and 15 percent of men and women of all ages say that they have no sexual desire. (See for example Nathalie Bajos and Michel Bozon, eds., L'Enquête sur la sexualité, pp. 489–490.) The older people are, the more easily they adapt to the absence of intimate relationships; the conjugal and sexual market is clearly less favorable for women over fifty, even if menopause no longer means the end of erotic activity (pp. 334 f.). On the other hand, the decline of desire begins for men ten years later, especially with the arrival of Viagra, which stimulates the libido. Half of those who are sexually inactive are fat or short (p. 342).

11. Cf. Nietzsche: "Thus the philosopher abhors marriage, together with that which might persuade to it—marriage being a hindrance and calamity on his path to the optimum. What great philosopher hitherto has been married? Heraclitus, Plato, Descartes, Spinoza, Leibniz, Kant, Schopenhauer—they were not; more, one cannot even imagine them married. A married philosopher belongs in a comedy, that is my proposition—and as for that exception, Socrates—the malicious Socrates, it would seem, married ironically, just to demonstrate this proposition." (On the Genealogy of Morals, trans. Walter Kaufman and R. J. Hollingdale, New York: Random House, 1967, third essay, section 7.)

12. Here we must distinguish traditionalist reactions to the emancipation of mores, for example the recourse to hymen reconstruction surgery for young women from North Africa who are can-

didates for marriage, which makes it possible to save face on the wedding night, from North American reactions, which translate an allergy to the promiscuity inherited from the 1960s. In the first case, the irony is that it is the most sophisticated techniques of microsurgery that enable young women to comply, at least in appearance, with the most noxious prescriptions of the patriarchal order. A great way of thumbing their noses at religious obscurantists! When will men be required to produce a certificate of virginity on their wedding day?

13. According to Abstinence Clearing House, a Christian conservative association, 1,400 purity balls are supposed to have taken place in the United States in 2007 alone. The ceremony has all the ingredients of a real marriage, with long robes, wedding cakes, limousines, and even wedding rings. Almost 80 percent of the girls are said to break their promise before they marry. Many of them, to avoid defloration, practice anal and oral sex and contract transmissible diseases because they lack information.

14. Report by Caroline Fourest and Fiametta Venner broadcast on France 2, "Envoyé spécial," February 28, 2008.

15. Edward Shorter, concerning Charentes in the eighteenth century, *Naissance de la famille moderne*, Paris: Le Seuil, pp. 74–75.

16. René Nelli, *L'Erotique des troubadours*, commentary by Octavio Paz, in *La Flamme double*, Paris: Gallimard, 1994, pp. 84–85. See also Denis de Rougemont's analysis in *L'Amour et l'Occident*, Paris: 10/18, 1995, pp. 78 ff.

17. See Jacqueline Pigeot's very fine book, *Femmes galantes, femmes artistes dans le Japon ancien*, Paris: Gallimard, 2003.

18. Michel Foucault drew on this paradox in developing his "repressive hypothesis" regarding Western sexuality in *La Volonté de Savoir*, Paris: Gallimard, 1976. He examines a society that crushes drives only the better to speak of them and manifests an endless discursive fascination with them.

19. Quoted in Jean Lebrun, *Le Pur Amour de Platon à Lacan*, Paris: Seuil, 2002, p. 159.

20. "You can collectivize your body," said magnificently Griselidis, a Swiss prostitute who died in 2005, "be for others and for yourself, become multiple like an alga mixed up with other algae. . . .

They can't be counted. Immense armies have passed over me. Waves and oceans of men who have passed over us, forests of pricks that have skewered us. But it's splendid." (Jean-Luc Hennig, *Grisélidis, courtisane*, Paris: Albin Michel, 1981, p. 140.)

21. The question already arises for handicapped people. In September 2006, the magazine *Reliance* looked into the political and ethical issues involved in providing sexual assistance for handicapped people and the training of aides in this area. (A series of articles organized by Catherine Agthe-Diserens and Yves Jeanne.)

22. Charles Fourier, *Le Nouveau Monde amoureux*, Geneva: Slatkine, 1984, p. 16.

CHAPTER 9. *Persecution in the Name of Love: Christianity and Communism*

1. Villiers de l'Isle-Adam, "La Torture par l'espérance," 1883. In *Contes cruels*, Paris: Les Oeuvres représentatives, 1993, pp. 21–29.

2. Quoted in Paul Veyne, *Quand notre monde est devenu chrétien*, Paris: Albin Michel, 2007, pp. 169–170.

3. Quoted by Benedict XVI, *Dieu est l'amour*, Paris: Cerf, 2006, p. 70, who asks us to believe in spite of God's silence.

4. Pascal, *Pensées*, ed. L. Brunschwicg, Paris: 1893; reprint, Hachette, 1961, § 553.

5. In his *Histoire de France*, Jules Michelet tells of an eighteenth-century marriage, duly approved by the Jesuits, between a young nun of the Visitation order, Marie Alacoque, and Jesus. This young woman, who was said to suffer from an overabundance of blood and had to be regularly bled, claimed to receive monthly visits from her Spouse, who merged his heart with hers and gave her celestial ecstasies. (Quoted in Roland Barthes, *Michelet*, Paris: Seuil, 1974, pp. 116–117.)

6. *De Utilitate Credendi*, quoted by Paul Veyne, *Quand notre monde est devenu chrétien*, p. 214.

7. Quoted in Frédéric Lenoir, *Le Christ philosophe*, Paris: Plon, 2008, pp. 151–153.

8. See Jean-Michel Rey's excellent analysis in *Paul ou les ambigu-ités*, Paris: L'Olivier, 2008.
9. Anders Nygren, *Eros et Agape*, Paris: Aubier, 1962, p. 64. Quoted in André Comte-Sponville, *Petit Traité des grandes vertus*, Paris: PUF, 1995, p. 368.
10. Saint Francis of Sales, *Traité de l'amour de Dieu*. In *Doctrines du Pur Amour*, Paris: Agora, 2008, pp. 33–34.
11. Quoted by Frédéric Lenoir, *Le Christ philosophe*, pp. 158–159.
12. For Islam, to love the God of love is a heresy, because a finite creature can love only what is finite. One must revere the Lord and fear him. Whence the persecution of the mystical poets, Mansur al-Hallaj, Ruzbihan Baqli, and Suhrawardi of Aleppo, troubadours of the supreme love for the Divine. (See Denis de Rougemont, *L'Amour et l'Occident*, Paris: 10/18, 1995, pp. 112–113.) For Mansur al-Hallaj, a Sufi mystic (857–922) put to death in Baghdad, see the magnificent translation of his poems by Louis Massignon, *Diwan*, Paris: Seuil, 1955, and his *Poèmes mystiques*, trans. Sami Ali, Paris: Albin Michel, 1998.
13. That was the attitude of Tiberine Trappists in Algeria, in 1996, and especially of their prior, Christian de Chergé, who, refus-ing to leave Algeria three years before his assassination by Is-lamists, saw his future assassin as his last friend: "And you, too, the friend of my last minute, who will not be aware of what you are doing, yes, for you too I want this mercy and this adieu envisaged for you. And let it be granted us to meet again, for-tunate thieves, in Paradise, if it please God, the Father of both of us. Amen! Inch Allah!" Treating one's murderer as one's friend, pardoning in advance his fatal act is a magnanimity too rare not to be emphasized. (Cf. Soeur Emmanuelle, *La Folie d'Amour, entretiens avec Sofia Stril-Rever*, Paris: Flammarion, 2005, pp. 125–126.)
14. Christianity uses and abuses a paradox that has been very suc-cessful: the last on Earth shall be the first in Heaven; those this world considers mad will be seen as wise in the other world; someone who wants to save his life will lose it; blessed are the poor in spirit, for they shall be celebrated in the beyond; one has to die for oneself in order to live in God; etc. This way of think-ing by antonyms (evil is a hidden good, poverty a secret wealth,

ignominy greatness by default) is above all a way of legitimating the status quo and never being caught short. Truth is always hidden in the contrary of the obvious. Thus murder can be seen as a proof of attachment, torture as concern for the other. This rhetoric's heritage proved very fertile in totalitarian regimes seeking to reeducate dissidents.

15. That is the meaning of Amos Oz's famous appeal with regard to the Israel-Palestine conflict: *Help Us to Divorce*, London: Vintage, 2004.

16. In her book on the French Revolution, Mona Ozouf offered two interpretations of this phenomenon: let us be brothers or I will commit suicide, and be my brother or I will kill you. (The latter is Chamfort's version.) The psychoanalyst Jacques André suggests a third interpretation: be my brother so that I can kill you on the altar of the nation. (Mona Ozouf, *L'Homme régénéré*, Paris: Gallimard, 1989, pp. 176–177).

17. *Doctrine du Pur Amour*, p. 88.

18. We have to make an exception for Rwanda, which was a genocide led by good Catholics against other Catholics in 1994, and in which many priests and prelates were involved. The Vatican's silence on this massacre, which compromised the whole Catholic hierarchy, is eloquent.

19. In Guatemala, the archbishop of the country had himself photographed with a rifle bullet in one hand and a birth control pill in the other in order to demonstrate their equivalence. In Chile, pro-divorce and pro-abortion demonstrators marched with signs addressing the Catholic clergy: "Get your rosaries out of our ovaries!" We recall Benedict XVI's diatribes in Cameroon in 2009, in which he accused condoms of promoting AIDS! The height of insanity was reached in an article in *L'Osservatore Romano*, the Vatican's official organ, dated January 3, 2009, in which a certain Pedro José Maria Simon Castellvi, president of the International Federation of Catholic Physicians, asserted that the pill had for years produced "devastatiing effects on the environment" due to the "tons of hormones" released into nature through the urine of women who were taking it. The pill was also supposed to be a non-negligible cause of masculine infertility! The final ploy of obscurantism is to call in the help of science.

20. Benedict XVI, *Dieu est l'amour*, p. 64.
21. *Libération*, October 15, 1998.
22. Vincent Cespédes, *Libération*, November 8, 2007.
23. *J'aime à toi*, Paris: Grasset, 1992, pp. 172–173.
24. Pierre Legendre, *Le Monde*, October 23, 2001.
25. André Breton, *L'amour fou*, Paris: Gallimard, p. 76.
26. Serge Chaumier, "Pour de nouveaux codes amoureux," *Libération*, February 14, 2001.
27. Michel Onfray, *Théorie du corps amoureux. Pour une érotique solaire*, Paris: Biblio-Essais, 2000, pp. 26–27.
28. Jacques de Guillebon and Falk van Gaver, *Le Nouvel Ordre amoureux*, Paris: L'oeuvre sociale, 2008, pp. 139–140.
29. Catherine McKinnon, quoted by Katie Roilphe in *The Morning After*, Toronto: Little, Brown, 1997, p. 141.
30. Andrea Dworkin, 1981, quoted by Lynn Segal in *Dirty Looks, Women, Pornography, Power*, London: BFI, 1993, p. 12.
31. S. Heck and P. Heck, *Les Joies de l'open marriage*, Montreal: Select, 1976, p. 160, quoted in Serge Chaumier, *La déliaison amoureuse*, Paris: Payot, 2004, pp. 294–295.

CHAPTER 10. *Marcel Proust's Slippers*

1. Emmanuel Berl, *Sylvia*, Paris: Gallimard, 1994, pp. 127 ff.
2. For example: "Love is more than ever to be reinvented, so much energy lost, hopes spoiled, souls disappointed. . . . How could we let people think that love is only what our time tells us it is? How can we accept such a degradation?" (Jacques de Guillebon and Falk van Gaver, *Le Nouvel ordre amoureux*, Paris: L'Oeuvre, 2008, p. 148.)
3. We recall the nun made famous by the media, Soeur Emmanuelle—a person of great merit, moreover—who devoted herself to the trash collectors in Cairo and is now in the process of being canonized. During broadcasts, she would shout to everyone present: "I love you, I love you."
4. One example among many: the sociologist Edgard Morin defining "a politics of civilization." Morin asks us "to exchange the hegemony of the quantitative for quality and for goods that can-

not be calculated, such as love and happiness" (*Journal du Dimanche*, December 28, 2008.)

5. This is the ambiguity involved in a certain charity that is far more love of poverty than it is a desire to help the poor emerge from their poverty. Some are delighted that there are poor people whom they can help; they become cockroaches feeding on the rubbish. Consider this very ambiguous remark made by Mother Teresa: "If only you knew how I sacrifice myself entirely in this absolute poverty. I await the handicapped, the paralytics, the incurables, I desire to become the spouse of Jesus crucified. It is not Jesus in his glory or in his cradle, but Jesus alone, naked, bleeding." Here, Christian masochism is combined with a kind of appetite for wretchedness that is supposed to shed an advantageous light on the person who combats it. The unfortunate are only an occasion for the beautiful soul to feel itself to be noble and to achieve salvation.

6. "Not for a moment have you ceased to be in my heart and in my mind. Not for a moment have I ceased to act in order to serve this magnificent France. This France that I love as much as I love you." (President Jacques Chirac's farewell speech, March 11, 2007.) For the record, let us recall that President François Mitterand's parting words in 1995—"I shall not leave you, I believe in the powers of the mind"—had another air and belonged to a different period, that of reserve.

Index